Praise for S

"A self-help classic."

—*Daily Mail*

"America's top relationship guide."

—*The Book Tribe*

One of "The 10 Most Iconic Relationship Books of the Past Ten Years."

—*Yahoo!*

"Men don't really go for 'nice.' They go for 'interesting.'"

—*Chicago Sun-Times*

"We're talking about having so much self-respect, Aretha Franklin would high-five you."

—*Los Angeles Times*

"The pejorative meaning of the word 'bitch' has been reclaimed . . . it means a strong, feisty woman who has moxie, and knows when to use it. A bitch is . . . sap free."

—*Pursuit Magazine*

"[Argov is] talking about a strong woman. Someone who knows what she's doing in life. Someone who will share the load, but who will stand her ground."

—Joy Behar, Co-host of *The View*

"Sherry Argov shows women how to transform a casual relationship into a committed one."

—*The Today Show*

"The Best of Culture."

—*Esquire*

WHY MEN MARRY

MARRY

Bitches®

WHY MEN
MARRY
Bitches®

A Guide for Women Who Are *Too* Nice

Sherry Argov

A DAVID & CHARLES BOOK
David & Charles is an imprint of F&W Media International, Ltd.
Brunel House, Forde Close, Newton Abbot, TQ12 4PU, UK

F&W Media International, Ltd is a subsidiary of F+W Media, Inc.
10151 Carver Road, Suite #200, Blue Ash, OH 45242, USA

First edition published in the UK in 2011
Reprinted in 2011, 2012, 2013

This edition first published in the UK in 2014

This edition is for sale in the United Kingdom and Ireland only, not for export
elsewhere.

A catalogue record for this book is available from the British Library.

ISBN-13: 978-1-4463-0475-4
ISBN-10: 1-4463-0475-2

Printed in Great Britain by TJ International Ltd, Padstow, Cornwall for:
F&W Media International, Ltd
Brunel House, Forde Close, Newton Abbot, TQ12 4PU, UK

10 9 8 7 6 5 4 3 2 1

crown © istockphoto.com / skodonnell
notebook paper © istockphoto.com / stockcam
lollipop © istockphoto.com / migin
baby items © istockphoto.com / bpowelldesign
bow © istockphoto.com / andres_
parchment © istockphoto.com / abzee and 123rf.com

F+W Media publish high quality books on a wide range of subjects.
For more great book titles visit: *www.fwmedia.co.uk*

For Mom, with love.

CONTENTS

Acknowledgments

First and foremost, I thank and acknowledge my beautiful mother, Judy. Aside from her being the best mother and my favorite person in the world, when I was growing up my mom taught me, by example, how to survive and stand on my own two feet in a man's world. To me, making my Mom proud is the only accomplishment that ever really mattered.

I also want to thank the amazing teams at Adams Media, F+W Media, David & Charles, and FWI, who are not only consummate professionals but also people who have become my friends. I thank David Nussbaum, CEO and President of F+W Media. David Nussbaum is such an extraordinary person, the kind of leader you might be fortunate enough to work with once in an entire career. I also want to extend much gratitude to Sara Domville, President of the Book Division at F+W Media, a diamond of a person. I thank Karen Cooper, the first female Publisher of Adams Media, and the best publisher in the publishing business. Creatively, Karen and I think almost identically; I value her advice immensely. I thank Chris Duffy, Royalties Manager at Adams Media, for being a consummate professional. Thank you for always going the extra mile. I thank James Woollam, Managing Director, for overseeing the release of this book. Thank you for doing such a magnificent job! I offer special thanks to Stephanie McKenna, Foreign Rights Manager at Adams Media, who is the reason this book is selling in so many languages.

I want to thank Edward Colbert of Looney & Grossman, who is my brilliant lawyer, and friend. Thank you, Ed, for being someone I can always depend on. I want to thank my accountant, Kathryn Schmidt of Schmidt & Co.

To my family and closest friends, my love. Since I don't want you to get harassed, I will leave your identities anonymous. Actually, there is only one spot open for a crazy lunatic to harass my family and friends (I've already filled it).

I want to also thank and acknowledge my readers. I have had the privilege and honor of meeting the most amazing and interesting women. Thank you for your support.

Introduction

Everyone's heard the story about the handsome prince who marries the average town maiden. Or the cute bachelor who could have any girl, but who falls in love with a difficult woman. At the wedding, the guy feels like he won the prize, instead of the other way around. Meanwhile, his family is choking on the wedding dinner, struggling to hold back what they are *really* thinking.

"Why doesn't anyone *else* like her?"

"Why did he pick her?"

At the reception, the speculation continues. "Is she pregnant? Is her belly showing? She must have a special hidden talent. Is it a sex trick? What could it possibly be?" What they'd love to do is pull the groom aside and ask him privately, "I don't get it. Why are you marrying this bitch?"

This is not another "how to fetch a husband" book. It's not a book that will perpetuate the false narrative "you are incomplete until you find your better half." On the contrary. This book is about self-worth, and confidence. This book will help you understand which qualities directly relate to how most men choose their eternal life partner. Why? For reasons men will explain in their own words.

When I use the word *bitch*, the woman I'm describing is not cruel or mean. Throughout this book, as well as in my first book, *Why Men Love Bitches*, I use the word *bitch* in a playful way. The title does not take the word *bitch* too seriously. I use the word *bitch* to describe a strong and competent woman, who has her own identity. She naturally gives a man his "space" because she has other aspirations and goals, and needs her own space. She will not accept disrespect. A woman with self-worth is what most men are *not* used to experiencing, and it stops them dead in their tracks.

We've all read Cinderella. We've seen the engagement ring commercials where the woman starts crying and jumping up and down screaming "yes" after a guy opens a black velvet box with bling-bling, and then pops the question. We've all attended weddings in which ten bridesmaids dress like prom queens. The women take photos with the bride and crouch over her, so they can stare adoringly at that big rock. Then comes the toss of the bridal bouquet, when all the single women trample over one another to catch the flowers. During the reception, the single women request Beyonce's hit, "If you liked it then you should have put a ring on it" and sing along like it's the national anthem.

Men see this behavior. They watch closely and they make immediate assumptions. It confirms what they already know. That marriage is the "holy grail" to most women.

Why is this a problem? It makes him fearful of her motivation for choosing him. In a guy's mind, a woman's desire for marriage doesn't necessarily mean she's madly in love with *him*. She is in love with a wedding fantasy. She wants her castle in the sky, and a princess happy-ending. She doesn't necessarily want the prince or love *him*. He is there to fill a position.

This is a concern that causes men to approach commitment cautiously. He wants to know a woman is interested in who he actually is. To a man, committing to a woman who is too hung up on the wedding fantasy is *entrapment*. Men aren't commitment phobic, they want real love also. But he wants a woman who wants him *for the right reasons.* She is a grown woman who knows how to TCB (take care of business). She's not a young girl with a girlhood fantasy.

There are many women figuratively sitting on the side of the road, waiting for their Bentley to pull up. There are others who are working hard to elevate themselves. Before a man will think about engagement, he has to think, "Gee it would be a cool thing to spend my life with her. She will help me navigate." And that doesn't happen when a woman acts like marriage is owed to her. Men don't share their observations while dating. Relationships don't come in neat little packages.

WHY MEN MARRY *Bitches*

That is why this book was written—to *translate* what men are thinking.

In the chapters you are about to read, you will learn what men told me. You will understand why he needs to wonder why you *aren't* like all the other women he meets. When you seem different, that's when the guy will think it is a privilege to build a life with you. You'll also understand how he *expects* you to react, and how you should *behave* instead.

The material in my books is not drawn on my experience (this is not an autobiography). The content is based on actual information I gathered from hundreds of hours of interviews with men. These men sat down and talked with me candidly and gave me a rare look at what men say privately to one another. Whether it's on the golf course or over a beer at a sports bar, there are certain attitudes about women, relationships, and marriage.

As long as I agreed to keep their identities completely anonymous, they gave me all the classified information I had set out to get . . . and more.

The intrigue . . . the mystery . . . the excitement . . . the suspense . . . this is all good natured. I write about what makes healthy relationships retain their "spark" or "spice" over the long haul.

The following chapters will teach you why doting on a man or bending over backwards to show "how much you care" is often the thing that leads him to believe you aren't interesting enough to pursue. You will learn why trying too hard won't bring you the love and attention you crave. You will learn why being independent and feisty earns a man's respect.

Perhaps you are married and want to spice things up. Perhaps you have no interest in marriage and prefer to stay single. This book is about how to have the love and respect from a guy who is worthy—so you have the power to choose any outcome you want.

If there is a special guy whom you are thinking about spending the rest of your life with, you will learn how to make slight adjustments in your behavior so you are viewed as that special girl he can't live without.

Before we start, I should give fair warning: This is not a G-rated book about sunshine and puppy dogs. It's not a "coddle your inner child" book. (I will talk to my inner child as soon as she's old enough to get a job and pay some bills.)

Now, take your shoes off and put your feet up. Go grab yourself a glass of wine or a cocktail. And remember to take everything I say with a grain of salt . . . with a slice of lime . . . and a shot of tequila.

Note: Throughout this book, names of men have been changed to protect the not-so-innocent.

1

THE ALLURE OF A
Strong Woman

His Checklist—What Most Men
Secretly Want in a Wife

*Beauty is how you feel inside, and it reflects in
your eyes. It is not something physical.*

~SOPHIA LOREN

The First Item on His Checklist: She Is Confident

Imagine a world in which roles were reversed and men behaved like women. Pretend that men cooked for women, picked up socks, wore painful high heels and sexy outfits—all because they couldn't wait to get married someday. Pretend you had a boyfriend who owned a hope chest with six black bow ties inside that he wanted his groomsmen to wear at his wedding. Imagine that he talked about wanting three kids each time a Pampers diaper commercial came on TV. Or that he greeted you at the door wearing silk boxers and cowboy boots, so he could do a pole dance for you. The next day at work, pretend that he sent a text with a naked photo of himself bending over and blowing you a kiss.

A few weeks or months later, assume this guy asked you questions like:

"Why are you always out with your friends?"

"Where is this relationship going?"

"Why don't you pay attention to me anymore?"

"Who was that other guy on the phone?"

"Is he better looking?"

"You never have time for me."

"Am I fat?"

"My biological clock is ticking."

"Why won't you marry me?"

By this point, you'd be thinking the guy is not firing on all cylinders. In other words, two scoops of crazy. Then you would give him the exit speech:

"It's not you, it's me. I love you but I am not in love with you. I am so busy with work. I know I will regret this one day but I can't see you anymore. I just don't have time for a serious relationship right now."

Then you'd be permanently "out of range." As in, your phone would be out of range. And the cell phone would have no signal.

As scary as it sounds, these are tactics women employ to get a man's attention. It works for a while . . . the relationship eventually implodes, and the woman had no idea what she did wrong.

Why do women do this to themselves? Women are blinded by the constant message that her sexuality is her currency to navigate through life. TV commercials and pop culture tell her how to behave. Do you wear high heels while mopping? Do you serve him ice-cold beer in trashy lingerie? Do you leave razor-sharp creases in his shirts like the employee-of-the-month? Are you gardening in stilettos? Are you wearing cellophane for him? Are you letting him spank you with a spatula? Are you fifty shades of desperate?

Desperation is the worst cologne a woman can wear, and most women are being told to bathe in it. Here's what a guy sees: a woman who is absolutely *terrified of losing him*.

Not surprisingly, when I interviewed men, these issues were obvious. They immediately said "confident women are in short supply." They repeatedly told me, "You want to marry a woman who is *different*. An individual. The one that does *not* act like other women."

DESIRABILITY PRINCIPLE 1

**In romance, there is nothing
more attractive than a woman who has
confidence in who she is.**

A man will consider a woman a long-term prospect only after she has added the key ingredients: respect and dignity. This is what makes a woman "relationship worthy" in his eyes. And for a guy to respect the girl, she has to throw out the rulebook of how she is "supposed" to act, and *think* independently.

Men want to see that you call your own shots and that you don't need input from anyone about how to put your socks on. The woman I affectionately refer to as a "bitch" is not mean. She is confident, and dances to the beat of her own drum.

If ninety-nine women go one way, she will set her compass bearings in her own direction, and not care whether he likes it or not. That will set her apart.

DESIRABILITY PRINCIPLE 2

The woman who is unforgettably sexy is a confident woman who can function on her own, and who won't always let him have the upper hand.

. . . with one caveat . . . she can't be so strong or combative that he feels emasculated.

It's important to be feminine physically, and to let him feel he is strong, but at the same time not to wear insecurity like it's an overcoat. Matt recalls a moment in which Jessica showed her confidence. On the third date, he made a playful comment to Jessica. He said, "You can't have me." It took her two seconds to playfully check him with a one-punch knockout. Her response: "Tell me why I should want you."

This didn't give him the "pick me, pick me" message. When you show that you aren't fearful of losing a man, he becomes fearful of losing you. "She's smart. This one is quality. I will need to show her my *finer* qualities to keep her interest."

In a music-channel documentary, Tim McGraw said something very interesting about his wife, Faith Hill:

"She's a straight shooter, that's for sure. She doesn't take any sh*t from anybody." She's beautiful and talented. This is what society celebrates. But at home? Her husband is proud of the attribute men respect most: a backbone.

DESIRABILITY PRINCIPLE 3

He needs to see you are smart and feminine, but that you don't need anyone else to think for you.

Faith Hill also said in a magazine, "As a woman, I sometimes have to repeat myself ten times in order to be heard." She didn't give in (nine times).

When a man sees that a woman is not trying to gain his approval and cares about her own self-interests also, he doesn't classify her as a mindless woman he can take advantage of.

Ashley is a good example of a woman who exudes this independence. One day, her new boyfriend gave his opinion on her clothing. She was ready to leave for a work-related meeting, and he told her to wear a dress instead of the pantsuit she had on. Then he told her she was wearing too much makeup. What most women would do is change the outfit. Instead, Ashley playfully told him, "Listen here, Versace. This outfit has always been fine. And I haven't had any complaints about the makeup either. But if you'd like, I'll let you know when I'm wearing this in advance. That way, if you don't want to see me in it, you don't have to come over."

DESIRABILITY PRINCIPLE 4
**Men handle you with more caution
(and respect) when they can't figure you
out and when they can't read you.**

The second he *doesn't* see emotion, excitement or all the transparent behaviors women show to gain approval, you become different and exciting. The less *readable* you are, the more he will make an effort. Now you are in a different category. You are the woman who is "different" than all the rest.

The Second Item on His Checklist: She Is Interesting

Think about the last time you were madly in love. Chances are, the guy wasn't perfect. He wasn't a billionaire with a private jet, six-pack abs, and he wasn't hung like a barnyard animal on Viagra. Chances are, he didn't satisfy you in bed five times before he rolled over and called it a night. But there was something sexy about him. Something . . . interesting.

Social media and magazines have set a standard, causing women to feel pressure to be perfect. They define what "perfect" is. We are told to have certain measurements. We are told what to wear. We are told to wear the perfect designer bag, and designer shoes. We are told to drive a prestigious car, and carry the latest model cell phone. We are told to eat kale and egg whites to keep that girlish figure.

If you ask a thousand guys their definition of "perfect" physically you will get a thousand answers. But you will get very consistent answers about character traits. She must be interesting . . . before he'll see "forever."

Here are the things he'll notice at dinner. "What does this girl have to talk about? Can I trust her? Will I be embarrassed if I take her to a corporate party?" If all she can talk about at dinner is shoes and makeup and which celebrity looks fat, he'll put her in a category: sex-buddy. To a guy, superficial values register on his radar as "me, me, me."

DESIRABILITY PRINCIPLE 5

One way to become much more interesting to a man on a date is to ask him intelligent questions about himself.

To a guy, interesting conversation does not include whether he wants kids . . . how much money he makes . . . or whether he sees himself getting married someday. It doesn't involve "feelings" or whether a celebrity is in rehab.

Instead, ask him about his business. Ask him about his work or his education. Ask him what he liked or disliked. Ask him what he defines as success. Ask him the most important thing he learned from a parent or relative. Ask him who or what inspires him to be great. These questions make him feel like a genius. Appear interested like you are learning something, and try to refrain from saying "Me too!" after everything he says. This is not about you . . . no . . . this is about *him* being a genius.

After he sees you are cute on the outside, he wants to know if you are beautiful on the inside. He wants to know if you are charming, trustworthy, exciting, smart, funny, and conversant on a number of different subjects (including **him**). The most important thing? *That you are not boring.*

DESIRABILITY PRINCIPLE 6

He doesn't marry a woman who is perfect.
He marries the woman who is *interesting*.

Beauty pageants are one example of how women are misled into thinking the most important pursuits in life are beauty tips and man-catching skills. It's the perfect example of the "me, me, me" behavior that men quickly get tired of. Everyone knows the losers want to strangle the winner, and the Southern Belle who wins Miss Congeniality is dying to tell the judges: "F*ck all, y'all." Nevertheless, they all insist they are earnest do-gooders for the poor. Or "goodwill ambassadors" for their favorite charity. When asked what they'll do if they win? It's always about the "little orphans."

MISS KANSAS:
"I am a junior pursuing a degree in pottery.
My dream is to visit third-world countries
and give every orphan a little flower pot."

MISS ARKANSAS:
"I will end world hunger. I want to help feed the starving,
the homeless, the unemployed, and the destitute.
That way all my relatives can eat."

MISS CALIFORNIA:
"My favorite charity is the blind little orphans
who are seeing-impaired. I want to give them
all designer Chanel sunglasses."

It would be more entertaining to strap them to a lie-detector test and ask questions about everyday life. Questions like, "Tell us about the hardest day you ever worked and what you did that day. Are you willing to ride the Greyhound bus so we can donate more money to the orphans? And finally . . . which one of these other bitches do you secretly want to smother with a pillow?"

The reality? Men don't pay attention to beauty queens until they report on the five o'clock news that one of them had a porn tape, a restraining order, or a drunk and disorderly arrest. Why? Now she's not perfect. To most men, perfect equals fake. And fake is boring. And boring means . . . she'll become as significant to him as a piece of furniture.

DESIRABILITY PRINCIPLE 7

**The fastest way to become boring to a
man is to try to be like everyone else.**

Many men believe that if a woman is too focused on what is on the outside, she is trying to overcompensate for something she lacks on the inside.

Men won't tell you this. In their endeavor to score as much sex as possible, they'll tell women the opposite. Men know women feel pressure to be perfect so they "throw them off the scent" with colorful stories to keep her focused on pleasing him (short term). Like the one about how all his ex-girlfriends are supermodels. Or the one about his ex having sex with him ten times a day. (Clearly, a figment of his imagination.)

To prove it's total nonsense, you can simply look at a photo of his ex. If it is true she had sex with him ten times a day, there will be visible signs. Her hair will look like something nested in it. Her ankles will be permanently affixed behind her ears. She'll have raccoon eyes. And after burning so many calories, she'll be so emaciated, someone will be throwing her a cheeseburger.

The media also tells women what "seductive" is. From movies and TV, you would think that the ideal sex fantasy is a woman who is jumping up and down on a pole, wearing a wig and a Little Bo Peep outfit. Is it interesting? If a man meets a woman who is trying too hard to please him or trying to fit an image, he is likely to think she is like every other woman . . . who is trying too hard.

In the beginning, he's looking to see what is interesting and unique *about her*. Men see the images women are told to believe and they start to feel like all the women he meets look alike, talk alike, think alike, and follow the same pattern. He wants to feel *different* in your eyes, and feel that you are *different* also.

If a woman is not unique in any way, he'll feel like she was manufactured on an assembly line with thousands just like her, pumped out of a factory in Michigan. Every girl would have a tattoo on her neck:

> **This bitch is made in Detroit.**
> **Serial number MI 56793566**
> **Shoes and bag sold separately.**

The good news? You can put away the Little Bo Peep outfit, the cheerleader outfit, the Mary Poppins outfit, and the sexy little schoolgirl outfit. Take it back to the children's store and get your money back. Besides, you had no right to wrongfully take it away from the poor 10-year-old girl who needed a Halloween costume.

To a guy, a woman can be beautiful, yet boring. He can have sex, but still think the woman he's having sex with is not interesting enough to pursue. Remember the scene from *American Beauty*? At the end of the movie Angela, the blond bombshell cheerleader, gets into an altercation with her dowdier friend, Jane. In front of Jane's boyfriend, the blonde bombshell says, "At least I'm not ugly!" Jane's boyfriend fires back very calmly: "Yes you are. And you are boring. And you are totally *ordinary*, and you know it."

Why? She thinks like every other woman, and she's not an individual.

Alex described why it can be a "constant headache" to be with a woman who is insecure. Here's what he said.

"An insecure woman who needs constant reassurance is exhausting. It saps all your energy. On a Sunday, you can't read the sports section while she works on her laptop. You have to focus 100% of your attention on her when she is in the same room. If you are sitting three feet away from her reading a book, she'll complain that you are ignoring her."

Alex's male colleague added, "Yeah . . . *highly irritating.*"

To a guy, quality time consists of sitting in the same room and relaxing with a woman he's in love with, even if they are both doing a separate activity. When a guy is madly in love, being together is exciting. If the chemistry is right, the girl would not need continual conversation. Without comfortable silence, he will never feel like he can recharge his batteries.

DESIRABILITY PRINCIPLE 8

A guy doesn't want to be the only reason a woman feels happy. It's a huge responsibility, and men hate responsibility.

This is why most men would prefer an attractive woman who is independent and perhaps rough around the edges, over an insecure woman who needs constant reassurance. If a woman is in charge of her own happiness, she won't tolerate disrespect including from him. And yes, men actually prefer this.

Michael J. Fox tells the story of how he met his wife, Tracy Pollan. They were taping an episode of *Family Ties*. He was a huge star in this TV series. While they were on set, after a lunch break, he walked over to Tracy Pollan and made a rude remark about her breath. "Man, did you have the scampi for lunch or what?" She immediately told him off, and then walked away. To this day he recalls, "I had a crush on her from that point on." They're married with four kids, and twenty-five years later he still talks about how beautiful he thinks she is.

It often happens that way. He disrespects her and she checks him. Something clicks inside him and she is suddenly taken much more seriously.

An insecure woman who is focused on image does the opposite. If a man ignores her, she seeks his validation and reassurance. She will choose a guy on a Harley with twenty tattoos and allow herself to be mistreated. He'll treat her poorly, then give her a half-baked apology on a voice mail. "Baby, I am sorry. I shouldn't have thrown you out of a moving vehicle at 30 miles per hour. Next time I will slow down to 10 miles . . . I promise.'"

Let's qualify. A worthless guy who likes insecure women wants to mistreat her so he can feel powerful. Why is he worthless? Because he has no moral compass. To him, cruelty is a *good* thing. (That alone makes him worthless.)

DESIRABILITY PRINCIPLE 9

A quality man will respect a woman who does not tolerate disrespect. This increases his desire and respect for her.

That doesn't require being combative or confrontational. It just means excusing yourself when someone is disrespectful, even slightly.

Steven told me about a gathering in which he introduced Kara to some guys on Super Bowl Sunday. Before the game started, one of the guys put his feet up and said, "Kara, can you bring me another beer from the kitchen?" Kara reached for her cell phone in the next room, and became distracted. Her boyfriend Steve said, "Hey man, are your legs broken? She's not a f*cking waitress." Steve recalls, "Had she fetched him a beer, I would have respected her less."

For a quality guy, if the woman is overcompensating, it will feel unnatural. Contrary to the 1960s black and white commercials showing women in an apron, this is not what men want. He doesn't want to marry his maid. This doesn't stimulate him or make him feel proud. A quality guy wants to marry a woman he respects as his equal. Therefore, no modern woman should meet a guy and immediately start acting like "employee of the month" at Jolly Roger motel.

If he's not a quality guy, that kind of "servitude" leads to other problems. "Fetch me a beer" will quickly lead to . . . "hey, baby, sit on my lap" and "hey baby, unzip my pants." The relationship will be on his terms. That's when a woman begins to feel she's being "taken advantage of." In a man's mind it's considered male entertainment. He'll kick back, crack a beer, and think, "She's trying so hard, I'll never have to break a sweat in this relationship."

DESIRABILITY PRINCIPLE 10

When a woman gives too much too soon, she sets the groundwork for a one-sided relationship.

In the movie *Confidence*, the lead character Jake says, "What you are looking for in a 'mark' is a person with weaknesses you can exploit." Whenever a woman needs approval and tries too hard to please a guy whom she barely knows, he will often exploit those weaknesses.

To be viewed as a partner, he's got to feel he's met his match or his psychological equal. Connor explained what men desire:

"I want to find a woman who is strong and independent so I can run things by her and get input. I want to know she'll carry her weight, make good decisions and give me a different point of view. I want her to surprise me . . . sometimes. If she has her own ideas and talents, and doesn't kiss my ass all the time, we will be a formidable team. She will make me stronger and help me grow a bigger empire." *

(*He is the big emperor.)

In other words, he can't control the woman mentally. That's why you hear men say that a mental challenge turns them on. He gets the mystery and excitement of not knowing what you are thinking all the time. If something is too easy—to a guy? It's boring. It's not a challenge. If something is slightly difficult, men are more stimulated and work harder to conquer it. If she doesn't sleep with him right away, and shows she has respect for herself, and she doesn't make her interest in having a relationship with him too obvious, she's more difficult. She is a challenge.

DESIRABILITY PRINCIPLE 11

When a man sees you are happy with him
but you can be just as happy without him,
he will take you much more seriously.

Men want you to continue to surprise or stimulate them
. . . mentally. When a man can't crack your code, profile you,
put a mark on you or figure out where your insecurities are,
you are no longer readable. You are not dependent. That's when
he doesn't have a 100 percent hold on you; you become sexy.
Independence makes you interesting and stimulating, rather
than boring. And that's when he will enjoy putting in his 50
percent share to win you over and keep your interest.

The Third Item on His Checklist: She Doesn't Need Me

In the movie *Closer*, Natalie Portman asks Jude Law why he
is so madly in love with the photographer, played by Julia
Roberts. "Is it because she's successful?" Jude Law quips,
"No. It's because she doesn't need me."

Women often meet a guy then change into whatever
she thinks he wants her to become. If he's Italian, she's
squashing homegrown tomatoes to make his favorite mari-
nara sauce. If he's a Grape-Nuts and berry-eating spiritual
type, she's eating berries with her morning chants and
sucking down wheat grass juice. If he's a member of a par-

ticular religion or cult, she accepts his beliefs. If he is an environmentalist, she sells her SUV and gets a hybrid, and cleans his toilet with vinegar.

It's almost as though she's asked herself, "Who are we going to be this time?"

Unless a guy is looking for someone to manipulate and control, he'll be much more drawn to a women who has her own interests, hobbies, and goals—because she doesn't need him to give her permission to be happy.

His perfect girl is not the one who says, "I like anything you like. I'll do anything. I will eat anything. I will drink anything. Whatever . . . I'm easy." Most modern men do not marry a Stepford Wife. "Yes, dear. Yes, dear. Whatever you say, dear."

DESIRABILITY PRINCIPLE 12

Every guy knows he can find a girl who is simply satisfied with satisfying *him*. They are much more turned on by a woman who cares about her own pleasure as well.

Countless men told me the same thing. One said, "There were a few women I dated but couldn't marry. They were always the women who were willing to drop everything and do anything I wanted." This includes with time, activities, and sex. Newsflash: if single men were to disclose this to women, they would never get laid.

It confuses women to see the way women are presented in the nude magazines for men, since the nude model talks about sports and sex, or things that please men. (I don't know about you, but I don't regularly sit on a bale of hay in the middle of a cornfield, butt naked, in order to catch a sunrise.) No matter how freezing it is, the model is sucking her finger while hanging upside down from a tree, and quoted as saying, "I love being naked, it feels so natural," even if she is in the middle of a snow blizzard, and went home with pneumonia. Then comes the G-rated literature (G is for garbage):

Turn-ons: Popsicles, Twinkies, and sunsets.
Turnoffs: People who don't like lollipops.
Favorite sport: Naked Bungee Jumping.
Most influential person in my life: My puppy.
Proudest accomplishment: Tying both shoelaces in less than five minutes.

Somewhere there is a boardroom of young girls with endless sugar-cookies who are told to come up with these ideas. "Hey kids, the winner of the writing contest gets a new tricycle!"

The message to grown women? You need him. He doesn't need you. Therefore you need to "dumb down," then please him at all costs, and take your clothes off as quickly as you can. It doesn't matter if you met him two days ago. If you talked about your favorite ice-cream, that's enough small talk. Time's up! Now get busy because it's your duty to satisfy him if you want to keep him coming around.

When choosing a sex-buddy? That's a winning formula. When choosing the love of his life? Nothing could be further from the truth. Many men said, "If my wife slept with me on the first date, I wouldn't have married her." Think about it. When a man comes home from a hard day's work, the last thing he wants to find is his wife naked on the front porch, licking a multi-colored lollipop, wearing her hair in pigtails, and watering the tulips.

He will assume you don't need him as much when you have other things that give you joy, and pleasing him is not your only goal. Troy explained very simply, "A smart, together guy won't marry a woman who has no interests of her own, and goals. He'll sleep with her, but he won't marry her."

Part of that is how quickly you jump into bed. But there are other indicators. Like when a guy asks you questions on a date . . . to figure you out. For example, he might ask something seemingly innocent like, "What do you like to do for fun?" He'll pay close attention. If you tell him *what* your hobbies or interests are, he will want to know *why* you like the hobby or activity. Next, he may tease you or challenge you, or give you a hard time about it. Why? Because he wants to see if you will vigorously defend your hobby or interest.

Brad tells the following true story about Cindy. They were on a date and Brad asked, "What do you do for fun?" Cindy responded, "I bought a high-end riding lawn mower.

Last weekend I had fun mowing my lawn." Here's what he observed: "She didn't care that I might think it's stupid or quirky. That is her thing and that's who she is. The fact that she was proud of it was a complete turn-on."

He wants to know if you can be happy . . . with him or without him and if you have your own identity. If so, he can exhale. "Whew . . . she doesn't need me."

DESIRABILITY PRINCIPLE 13

When you are happy, you are sexy.

Another variation of "what do you do for fun" is when he asks you to choose a restaurant on the first or second date. The reason he wants you to choose where to eat is he is worried you won't like the place he picks. If he chooses a place that is not fancy enough, he's afraid you'll think he's too stingy. If the place is too expensive, he's worried you'll think he's too eager or desperate, and that he is *trying too hard* to impress you. So he puts the ball in your court.

Men have two chief complaints about how women respond. The first is obvious—she chose the place that was too expensive, and then didn't eat the food. The second complaint is less obvious. She was too indecisive about the restaurant, and couldn't choose a place. That can be viewed as a sign of weakness.

It's one of the things men see as weakness: ***indecisiveness***. It's a flaw that ranks almost as high as whining and nagging.

Eric gave me a quasi re-enactment. He said:

"If a woman cannot make a decision about a restaurant, she won't be able to make any other decisions. In ten years, I will ask her 'Honey, who is picking up the kids from school?' (Then he changed to a high-pitched woman's voice.) She'll tell me, '*I don't know who is picking up the kids, honey. I will leave it up to you. You decide. By the way, where are the kids? I haven't seen them since last Thursday.*'"

If men could rewrite the wedding vows, they would go like this:

"Do you promise not to nag, whine, or bring things up from the past?

♥

Do you promise to appear reasonably logical some of the time?

♥

Will you share your opinion when I ask for it?"

If man is trying to assess what kind of mother a woman will be, decisiveness is a major clue. A "whatever" girl is the same as a "yes" girl. Therefore,

DESIRABILITY PRINCIPLE 14

If a woman is indecisive about little things, he will see it as a sign of weakness, and an indicator that she won't be able to make more important decisions later in life.

After you pass the "what do you do for fun" hurdle and the "you choose the restaurant" scenario, the probing will continue. For example, he may walk out of a horrible movie with you and then ask you what you thought of the movie. If you say, "Great special effects!" he'll respect you a little less. It is better to say, "Good company. But the movie sucked." When a man can see you shoot straight and speak your mind, he will view you as a more legitimate candidate.

Thomas described what it feels like to be with a woman who is indecisive, has no identity, and offers no mental challenge. She simply tries to agree with everything he likes. Thomas said, "It's like playing tennis with yourself. You keep hitting balls over the net, but no balls are coming back."

Men used different words, but said the same thing. The pressure becomes unbearable for a man when a woman is overrun by obsession with the relationship, or pleasing him. When her whole worldview boils down to him, it quickly becomes boring.

If he will see you as potential "wife" material, he wants to see if he can confide in you, throw out ideas at you, and get a different point of view. He does not think you have all the answers (that's his job). But if you challenge him with questions and make him see other angles, he will see you as partner material.

Later when you are married? He'll still want your opinion. A couple of different things may happen. Either he will take your advice and tell everyone it was his brilliant idea or he will decide that he was right all along (and you were wrong). Either way, he'll appreciate the input because you helped him realize . . . he is right!

Men assume the woman is weak, sprung, or obsessed when she stops giving her opinion and becomes afraid to say, "No, I don't want to do that." Or, "No, I don't like that." Or, "Yes, I like this." Or, when she doesn't feel good about herself, unless he tells her she's worthy. Confidence begins when you . . .

DESIRABILITY PRINCIPLE 15

Don't believe what anyone tells you about yourself.

Here's another secret men shared and it's a highly classified secret he doesn't want you to know . . . . It is a man's world so men are used to getting their way. When a woman has her own way of doing things, she becomes very intriguing to a guy. That's when a guy will think, "Gee, she has a special magic about her." What is the magic trick? She can tell him to go jump in the lake whenever she feels like it.

Even though a guy might seem a little annoyed when he doesn't get his way, he'll secretly respect it. Suddenly, he'll get to see things from a different perspective. And then he'll start thinking about how he can fit into . . . *her* spicy world.

2

MAKE HIM CHASE

You

UNTIL YOU CATCH

Him

How to Convince Him Commitment Was *His* Idea

When women go wrong, men go right after them.

~MAE WEST

Changing the Game

You can't wrestle a man down like a wrangler at the rodeo and hog-tie him to get a commitment. Just like the little calf, he'll run to get away from you. Instead of trying to lasso or hook a guy, you have to change your approach. When it comes to commitment, he hooks himself. All you have to do is be feminine, soft, charming, and enjoyable to be around. Then toss him the rope. Watch. He'll get all tangled up in it.

Deep down, men want to be chivalrous. They want to have a woman they can cherish and do everything for. Just like a woman's instinct is to please, a man's instinct is to pursue. He wants you to think he is dark, smoky, and mysterious like James Bond. He wants to feel he's working his spell on you, and you are taken by him. But . . . not *too* easily taken. He wants to win you over . . . *incrementally*.

DESIRABILITY PRINCIPLE 16

Men like to be curious. They like to feel that there's more to the story than what they already know.

Robin is a perfect example of a woman who tried to accelerate this process. Mike wanted to take her to dinner on a second date, but she insisted on cooking instead. When he came over, he encountered a five-star production. Robin served foie gras, the finest goose-liver pate in the world. When he reached for the salt, she started apologizing. "My cooking is usually better than this." What Robin divulged is that she cares too much . . . and too soon.

Here's Mike's take: "After foie gras, I know I'm getting laid. And I know she wants a ring on her finger. But if she throws me a sandwich or a sloppy joe, that means I still have something to prove. When I'm not quite sure *how much* she likes me, that's when the challenge is on."

DESIRABILITY PRINCIPLE 17

If you let on that you are insecure about winning him over, he will know he has you. And if he knows he has you, it's unlikely you will engender that overwhelming feeling of attraction that is necessary for him to want to marry you.

Once it's obvious you are *totally* 100 percent hooked, there's nothing exciting about you anymore.

More to the point, did it sound like a fun evening for Robin? Always assess the work-to-fun ratio. If you add grocery shopping hours, cooking hours, and cleaning hours in the kitchen the day after he leaves, the work-fun ratio for

Robin and her foie gras was 10:1. In other words, ten hours of work for less than one hour of pleasure (and with some men, the fun only lasts three minutes).

My friend Ashley had a better work-fun ratio. She had a date with one guy on a Friday and they went out for Chinese food. They tried several dishes and had plenty of leftovers, so Ashley took home all the doggie bags. The following evening, she had a date with a different guy and decided to be the "hostess with the mostest." She reheated the Chinese leftovers, "reorganized" a medley on a pretty plate, and served it to her guest of honor. Total time expended? Three minutes. Total fun? Five hours of fun, two days in a row, totaling ten hours. (Much better ratio.)

The fortune cookie said: "The catered din-din was a smashing success."

DESIRABILITY PRINCIPLE 18

The mental challenge is not, "Can I get her to sleep with me?" The mental challenge is, "Can I get *and keep* her attention?"

A man taking on a new relationship is like a young boy opening a new jigsaw puzzle for the very first time. If he opens up the box and the puzzle is already put together, all the fun and excitement is taken out of it. But if the kid has to think, imagine, strategize, and put all the little pieces together, his mind is being stimulated. And then the little boy is tickled pink.

When it comes to securing a man's interest in commitment, your best strategy is to behave as if you like him, but you *aren't* that interested in locking him down. The objective is not to be standoffish, just low key. The lower the profile, the more he'll come in for the kill. And by "low profile" I mean, appear happy to see him, just don't *assume the role of his girlfriend.* When you don't step into that role, he'll lower his guard and begin to pursue *you.*

The reason for this is that men are programmed to protect their freedom. He starts off halfway suspicious that you want to get married to begin with. So the minute you start talking about commitment, hinting about marriage, or appearing to want to take him down, he'll "do battle" to fight for his freedom. The second you utter words like *monogamy, kids,* or *minivan,* he'll put up a wall. In his mind, every woman is looking for a "live one" so she can plot his capture . . . arrest . . . and future life in captivity.

Ever wondered why men read women's magazines? They're spying on the opposition. A man will read all the articles like "How to Get Him to Commit Even Though He Slept with Your Little Sister and Cousin with Buck Teeth." They always show a picture of a guy with his back turned to a pouty-looking woman wearing a ninety-dollar bra. So he figures, "All women have a preset agenda."

DESIRABILITY PRINCIPLE 19

As soon as a man has his guard up, he will not fall in love or get attached.

What makes matters even worse is all the horrible advice about how a woman should verbally "negotiate" a relationship. Whether it's exclusivity in the beginning or getting engaged a year later, the conventional wisdom is to put your cards on the table and tell him you want a relationship (as if he doesn't already know). In other words, get busy on the fast track. This, the so-called experts say, will save time and cut to the chase so you can know going in whether or not he's "marriage minded." Right? Not so fast.

Men have a name for this. They call it "the talk." It's the first sign of trouble. Here are some of the things women say during dinner conversation or pillow talk within the first couple of months. It's the fastest way to put a guy at ease and tell him he has the upper hand:

The Dreaded "Talk"

- Where is this headed?
- What do you see in the future?
- How do you feel about commitment?
- I'm looking for the one.
- Do you want to settle down?
- I refuse to waste my time in a dead-end situation.
- I'd like to have children.
- Do you ever see yourself getting married?
  Or remarried?
- Do you want kids? How many?
- I am looking for security.
- What are you looking for?
- My clock is ticking.

They see it as a trap because it's being offered to him willingly. In Russia, there is a motto: "Free cheese you will only find in a mouse trap."

The woman thinks she's subtly beating around the bush, or helping to move things along. But to a guy? He sees this as *way too obvious*. It's as blatant as a farmer opening up the mouth of a work mule to examine the teeth: "Good stock! I'll take him."

DESIRABILITY PRINCIPLE 20

Your power gets lost the minute you start asking, "Where do I stand?" Because what you've just told him is that the terms of the relationship are now *his to dictate*.

If it happens too soon, he will usually feel he's being coerced into a plan that is no longer his. Even one or two of the above questions and . . . *poof*!

- Alarms will go off,
- His guard will go up, and
- He'll start planning his escape
- He just won't show it (until after he sleeps with you)

He may stick around for three months, or he may exit after six. But if you've told him you won't "waste your time in a dead-end relationship" or that you want to be married within one year, all you've done is tell him you're someone he needs to get away from. This is why being up front and "open" doesn't work.

DESIRABILITY PRINCIPLE 21

He needs to see that you are smart, but that you aren't talking.

The only way he'll get attached is if you lower his guard first. It's similar to how women approach casual sex. If a guy hits on you in a bar and comes on too strong, chances are you'll think, "It's hardly a compliment. He's so horny, he'll shack up with anything in a skirt." Because the guy is being so obvious, your guard immediately goes up and you want nothing more to do with him. Right?

This is exactly how men approach commitment and marriage. They feel like most women would marry a toothless ex-convict as long as he got on bended knee and told her she had a pretty hairdo. So, the second you bring it up, or you seem too fixated on securing a serious relationship from the jump start, you get categorized as having "a plan" or "an agenda." And then his interest in anything long term will go right out the window.

DESIRABILITY PRINCIPLE 22

When a woman rushes in too quickly, a man will assume she is in love with a "fantasy" or the *idea* of having a relationship. But if he has to slowly win her over, incrementally, he'll think she's falling in love with *who he is*.

To him, a vacant "boyfriend slot" or an open "husband position" looks about as desirable as stepping into an open bear trap. He wants to feel like he won a special girl who isn't easily obtained. And no guy feels that way if she comes across as having an opening that was available before he even got there.

Eddie explained, "My ex-girlfriend told me, 'Most men would jump at the chance to marry me. And if you don't marry me, I might end up marrying one of your friends.' That's like a guy saying to a woman, 'If you don't bang me, I'll get one of your girlfriends to do it.' Women say that stuff about marriage all the time and have no idea how it comes across."

In his mind, you are cheapening the relationship. You want a husband quickly, but you don't necessarily want quality. That makes him feel like an ordinary chump. And everyone wants to feel like they are special.

Joking with a guy doesn't make your motives any less obvious. Allison is a perfect example. She and Jamie had been out a few times, and one night they had a few too many drinks. She looked at him and jokingly said, "Am I just a piece of ass, or do you have feelings for me?" What this says to a guy is that she has low self-esteem. If she knows she's not a piece of meat, she would never ask that question.

Another guy told me a story about a woman who said at the end of the first date, "If you kiss me, you are going to have to marry me." She thinks she's being cute or funny. It's not cute to a guy.

During the dating, no jokes about marriage, babies,

commitment, and serious subjects. If you want to blow him away . . . say nothing. Rule number one: You have to be coy. You have to come at him in a different way than what he's used to encountering. This includes what you say. It also means you can't be too obvious with your facial expressions.

DESIRABILITY PRINCIPLE 23

**Don't even mention the word *commitment*.
That's the whole trick. The less you say about it,
the closer you are to getting one.**

In fact, each time you say "commitment," you've just added on a few weeks or months. And don't talk about exclusivity or monogamy. The less you ask, the more he'll tell. All negotiations should be 95 percent nonverbal and 5 percent verbal. You have to act like you are still getting to know him, and that commitment is nowhere on your radar.

This will disarm him. Now he's a warrior without a battle plan because he has no idea how to swing his ax. With the nice girl, he can see what her plan is and win. But with a bitch, he *can't* see his opponent or her plan. This is precisely why he plays . . . right into her hands.

In the movie *Training Day*, Ethan Hawke is having a discussion with his training officer, played by Denzel Washington. They are discussing survival skills. He said: "Don't show your smiles or your cries."

Now, let's practice. Let's pretend you are on a date. Imagine that you are sitting in his car under the moonlight, kissing. While he's putting on the moves he asks, "Where do you see yourself in five years? Do you see yourself getting married?" (Not that he cares. He just has to pretend he's interested in a "meaningful relationship" in order to hit the target.) So you answer, "Oh, yes. I see myself married, with two kids. One boy and one girl." And worse yet, she's grinning like a possum. (Cut!!! Wrong answer. Let's rewrite that script and reshoot this scene.)

You have to hit the Snooze button on your biological clock. Remember, "Don't show your smiles or your cries." If a man asks you a direct question about marriage or kids, you have to deflect the question with one of the following:

"Marriage? Who, me?
I suppose if I found someone special
enough I'd consider it.
But he'd really have to be pretty amazing."

"It hasn't crossed my mind.
I guess it would depend on the person
and how we felt about each other."

In other words, act about as enthusiastic as you'd be if he asked you what size engine you have in your car.

The point is to give him *no guarantees* before he has earned it. If he says, "You are my only girl," that's called lip service. He earns it when he shows you he consistently treats you well over a period of months. (Deeds, not words.)

Until then, be sure to interject his favorite word: *fun*.
Used in a sentence:

"We are enjoying each other and having fun."

"I think the world of you."

Here's how the word *fun* translates in the male brain:

No pressure. No expectations. No demands.

At the end of a date, avoid asking, "When will I see you again? When will you call me?" Instead, play up your femininity. Smile, give him a kiss, thank him, and tell him how much you enjoyed yourself. Then be sure to kick him out. Don't forget the magic word: *fun*. He is a "really fun guy." This lets him know you live for the moment. And you correlate time together with being treated well.

After several dates, if he asks, it is fine if you *hint* or imply that there is no one else you are sleeping with. First, he has to appear sincere and consistent on his end and take you out a few times. Second, he has to give you the same assurance and inquire whether you are seeing anyone else. Don't offer or bring it up first. A little reassurance keeps him in the game. But as for what you see in your future? (Oops.) You can't see past next weekend.

To a woman, this seems like torture or a cruel circus trick. But for a man, this is relationship Nirvana, Utopia, and a wet dream come true with Wonder Woman. Suddenly, he can relax and enjoy himself. "Wow. That's pretty cool. Finally, I can get closer to a woman without pressure. I don't have to worry about her locking me down." Now you become that cool dream-woman he's always heard about, but has never met. *Then he lowers his guard and falls in love.*

Therefore, on a date, talk about everything that interests you. Just don't be all up in his grille about relationships, "the future," kids, or marriage.

The opposite is also true. If you never want to go out with a guy again, keep talking about your biological clock. Tell him the fertility doctor said your eggs are popping all over the place. Say "ooh" and "ah" over every newborn you see strapped to a woman's chest. Tell him you want lots of kids, your religion prohibits the use of birth control, and your mom is moving in to help take care of the little ones. (Less expensive than a restraining order, and far more effective.) To seal the deal, buy a card and leave it on his doorstep with a baby rattle and a Winnie-the-Pooh stuffed animal (the kind that plays sappy lullabies if you wind it up). Then write, "I can't sleep or eat. I think about you constantly. I can't wait to begin our future together." (See Charlie? See Charlie run . . . .)

The Bitch Convinces Him He "Won" the Commitment

It's one thing not to offer guarantees, but it's something altogether different when two to three months have passed and you still seem slightly unsure how he fits into your future. You should continue to be very sweet. That will confuse him because he'll be asking himself, "Wait, why isn't she pressuring me for a commitment?" At some point he'll bring it up. A good thing to say is:

"I really like you but I'm not 100 percent sure. We are still learning about each other."

His immediate response will be, "You aren't sure? What do you mean you aren't sure? I am the brightest, the 'bestest,' and the smartest!" No guy that thinks he's winning will accept defeat willingly. So he'll automatically step up his game to win you over. Why? To prove he is a worthy pick. And then you get a twofer. Not only do you get commitment . . . you even convince him that it's *his idea*.

DESIRABILITY PRINCIPLE 24

If he has no guarantees, becomes attached, and thinks you could be gone at any time, that's when he'll cherish the idea of securing a relationship.

He might become suspicious that other men are pursuing you. And it's good for him to wonder a little. But you should never talk about other men directly. Just be unavailable once in a while, and it will automatically turn the cogs in his imagination.

The reason keeping a little bit of distance makes a man fixate on you is that nine out of ten women *assume the role of girlfriend after a month or two*. Sometimes even *a week or two*. First, she starts calling him for his nightly bed checks. Then his socks are rolled up into little balls, and his closet is reorganized. His weekends are filled with weddings, open houses, and baby showers. And before long, he starts to miss football Sundays on the couch with his hands down his pants (to make sure he's still got 'em).

This is why men back off. The adjustment is too drastic, too quick, and too easy. Like he's joined the army, his hair has been shaved off and he has no idea who he is anymore. Now he's no longer "the man." Now he is Bambi in the crosshairs, and the crosshairs are aimed right at his little Bambi balls. So he scurries out the door . . . like he's being shot at.

Remember, you want to discuss commitment, but he does not. Commitment is something a man has to fall into. It's sort of like falling into an eight-foot-deep hole in the ground that he didn't see coming until it was too late. He went out for a nice little stroll and oops . . . lo and behold . . . he fell. "Help! I've fallen and I can't get up!" Now he's stuck to the floor like a peanut butter cup.

DESIRABILITY PRINCIPLE 25

There's nothing more prized to a man than something he had to wait for, work for, or struggle a little bit to get.

. . . because he thinks few others could get it, and he did, therefore he is "special."

Men are natural-born competitors. In poker, they keep a poker face. In business, showing emotion is "wimpy." Whether it's sports, games, or a business negotiation, if the one player has a weakness, the other person can discover it and get the upper hand. Young boys say "I beat you" on the playground. Grown men say in business, "Don't accept defeat." Everything is a strategy or competition. Likewise, if you go down in the first round, he doesn't feel you will be a worthy sparring partner. And, every other guy could take you as easily.

The irony is, when he *doesn't* have you, that's when he thinks the whole relationship is being dominated by him and he's in control of "where it's going." To him, dominance is about getting the woman he really wants. Entrapment is about getting hog-tied by a woman who chose *him*. The latter is emasculating. This is why you want to remain "dumb like a fox" and allow him to think he's in control. Here's how.

How to Convince Him He Is a Winner . . . Almost

- Begin by seeming as if you don't want to hang on to him too tightly. In his mind, this means he isn't "wonderful" . . . yet.

- Then give a little encouragement, but not too much. The best way to do this is with strategically placed compliments. "You are so smart." Now he thinks you admire him, but he's dominating the relationship and is in control of "where it's going."

- Be sure to say, "I really value your opinion. Could I ask your advice?" He will then take a full hour to show you how "manly" he is. No yawning allowed; simply order another drink.

- Be affectionate in public. Touch his lower back when you are waiting in line at the movies. Stand close to him here and there. Touch his hand at dinner. Rub his knee while he's driving, because then his hands are busy on the wheel or the gearshift. Don't do it excessively—just a little. And try to keep sex at bay.

- When he becomes a little more aggressive, don't respond in a "hot and heavy" way. If he gropes your butt or tries to put his hand close to the twins, give him a little bit of play but not too much. Then you can say, "Let me come to you." It's every guy's fantasy: having a woman jump his bones. He'll be patient as long as he feels he's not wasting his time, and can see a light at the end of the tunnel.

- If he kisses you and you respond with "oh baby, oh yes," then he reads it as "She is ready for mounting." But if, instead, you remain cool when he's putting on the moves, then he has to question what it is that you want.

- That's where you want to keep him because now he's thinking of how to please you and win you over.

- The longer you keep him in a suspended state of not knowing if he's won you over, the more he'll cherish you and the more attached he'll become.

When a man is in pursuit mode, he gets the same rush he gets when he's playing a slot machine in a casino. He can lose ten times in a row, but he'll still be on the edge of his seat thinking, "I'm almost winning." No guy wants to willingly accept defeat. Every time he thinks he's losing, all you have to do is sweeten the pot. If you ask him to fix something, he feels like a winner. If you convince him he had a great idea, he's a winner. If he suggests a shoot-'em-up-bang-bang movie or auto racing, and you say "No, I'm not going," and then twenty minutes later you say "You are right, let's go to an auto race," now he's winning again. He thinks he's dominating the whole show—as long as you make everything *his* "brilliant" idea. He even buys a big fat engagement ring for this reason. Why? So other men will look at the ring and say "I can't compete with that." Now he's a winner again.

Liz and Matt were at a romantic Italian bistro, six months into their relationship. Before dinner was served he said, "Look, I'm not ready for anything too serious. How about you? Do you want to get married?" She came back with a great answer. "Gee, I can't tonight. My dress is at the cleaners and I have to be up early in the morning. But I'm so flattered. Thank you for asking." (A year later, he got up and told that story to the guests at their wedding.)

When a man is left guessing what you want, it makes commitment desirable because he has a chance to bring it up. He also doesn't have to worry, "Is she in love with me, or is she in love with the fantasy?" This is a huge consideration in the commitment equation for a guy.

On the other hand, if you seem to encroach, or drop not-so-subtle hints that you are "entitled" to a relationship, he'll go into a stall pattern. Or a "holding pattern." A holding pattern means that something has the *appearance* of movement but it really isn't making any headway.

Visualize an airplane that is taxiing on a runway, going around in circles, but never takes off. This is what men often do in relationships. They create the appearance that there is progress in the relationship, while putting it on ice. And you sidestep this by *not making it obvious* you want a "meaningful relationship," and by carefully observing his actions. At the same time, ignore what he says.

Because this is so important, let's do a recap of the typical dating dynamic, so you recognize the trap you shouldn't be stepping into.

WHY MEN GET SPOOKED OUT OF WANTING A COMMITMENT

First, he meets a woman he likes a lot. Her independent and slightly elusive aura gives him an important first impression:

"She doesn't need me. She likes me for who I am. Let me get to know her better."

So far so good. If she starts probing about "his intentions" or "the future," he will say:

"Let's get to know each other slowly and see where it leads." Or, "Let's take it one day at a time."

Women will sometimes misinterpret this as rejection. Then she begins to press for more verbal reassurance:

"Where is this going?"

"What do you see in our future?"

"Where do we stand?"

(Now let's hit the Pause button.) Here's why you won't get the response you're looking for. If he's operating on his own time clock, commitment or exclusivity will be something he'll bring up after three to six months. Most women don't wait that long. They bring it up after two to four weeks. A man must feel desired *for who he is* before committing, and in his mind you can't possibly know him well enough after a couple of weeks to make that decision. It has nothing to do with seeing other women or "commitment phobia." He wants to feel it's his unique set of qualities you fell for, and that his "magnificence" and "brilliance" won you over. And that you wouldn't be with just any guy who would take you in. This is the number-one reason why men back off. This is why you need to seem as if you haven't made up your mind. He wants your search to be complete and thorough, because you are discerning and will not settle for second best. If you are in a hurry, he'll think:

> **"She's insecure and needs to fill a void.**
> **She cannot be alone."**

> **"I'm just filling a position.**
> **She needs me to write checks for her dreams."**

> **"Her attention or desire to secure a relationship has**
> **nothing to do with me personally."**

That's when the holding pattern and stall tactics begin:

> **"Space. I need space."**

> **"I'm very busy with work."**

> **"My circumstances need to change before I can commit."**

"It's nothing you did, it's all me.

I fell off my bike in the third grade, and my unresolved childhood issues prevent me from committing.

My therapist tells me that too much intimacy would be harmful to my emotional healing."

"I'm just not ready . . . right now. But I may feel differently in six to nine months. In the meantime, I could use a little convincing, preferably while naked [pants unzip]. Right here . . . ooh . . . yeah, that feels good. Don't stop . . . ."

Anytime you "lobby for a position" or try to move things along, the guy will be reticent to shift gears. This is true after three months or three years. At every interval, you have to make it his idea. Men are hunters. And he has to chase you . . . until you catch him.

Shawn and Theresa are an example of what often happens six or nine months down the road. They were seriously involved for almost a year. He had been married previously. The ex-wife was remarrying and vacating his Bel Air home. Shawn told Theresa he was thrilled to be moving back into his beautiful house. That Sunday, he drove her by the house to show it to her. As they passed it, she instantly blurted, "When you move back in, I'm moving in with you!" Until then, Shawn had been thinking along the same lines. But when she said that, it made him want to move farther away from her, in the opposite direction. In his mind, it was his decision to make. Not hers.

DESIRABILITY PRINCIPLE 26

**As soon as a woman hands a man a
more serious commitment on a silver platter,
he'll be reluctant to take it.**

This is why you often hear of how men freak out over
a woman leaving her toothbrush or a hair dryer at his place.
Like in the movie *How to Lose a Guy in Ten Days* or in the
saga of Carrie and Big in *Sex and the City*. There are several
things women do to "move things along" that men regard as
dead giveaways. Women see them as innocent, but men see
them as glaringly obvious. When I interviewed men, they
said they pick up on even the most subtle nuances. The following list is based on the feedback they gave:

- **Don't introduce him as your "boyfriend" right
  away.** This suggests to a man that you are setting
  up for the long haul, and you want to preserve the
  impression you are still undecided.
- **No lover's gazes.** To you it's romantic. But to him,
  he's being eyed up like prey no different than the
  way a lion looks at a gazelle. If you've ever seen a
  lion look at a gazelle, it hides in the bushes and stares
  down the gazelle. That's how men feel when you do
  the goo-goo eyes too soon.
- **With voice messages, shorter is better.** And don't
  profess your love from the mountaintop. Something
  familiar or too cozy like, (Beep!) "Hi, pooky wooky

I just called because I miss you." Or, "Hi . . . it's just me," or, "You know who this is," after one or two dates can set off bells and whistles. Why? Because of the automatic presumption that you two are already an item. When you leave a message, say your name and your number as though it's the first (and last) time you could be calling. This translates as: unobtainable.

- **If you are on a dating website, don't let him know.** If you meet someone through the dating site, make sure your ad is very nondescript and reveals very little about you. You are well rounded, have a couple of hobbies, and want to meet a "a friend to do fun things with." Don't write that you are "tired of the dating scene" or advertise that you are looking for heavy romance. Don't list your interests as "enjoy strawberries covered in chocolate, walks on the beach, romantic getaways." If he reads that you like these things before he has met you, it won't feel authentic or special if you do it with him. Your ad should not say you are looking for "Mr. Right" or that you "love children."

- **With text messages, 1–2 short sentences is the maximum.** Think of the limit as the same as Twitter, where you have a limit on words. Text him the way you would your co-worker (if you are running late, or confirm plans). Tell him you hate texting, so he gets into the habit of calling you and seeing you.

- **Don't give him framed pictures of you for his home and office.** And no shots fired through the ex-girlfriend's photos, either. For proper disposal of all ex-girlfriend memorabilia, simply wait until you move in together. Between pickup and the scheduled delivery, boxes marked HANDLE WITH CARE shall mysteriously disappear to the dump.

- **Do not leave this or any other relationship book on a table or anywhere he can find it.** If he asks, you don't read trashy romance novels. You don't read relationship books. Hide this book like it's illegally smuggled contraband.

- **Don't mark your status on Facebook as "in a relationship" with a heart and a happy face, and his photo.** Men think there is only one reason women display the relationship on social media—to mark him as your "territory."

- **Don't mention his family or bring him over to meet yours until he gets serious with you.** You have no guarantees that your family won't give up too much information. Your brother will say, "I like this one better than the other loser." Your mom might ask when the wedding is. Your dad might add, "After all, you are no spring chicken!" Your grandma will think you are already married and say, "Tell your nice husband to go get me some applesauce."

- **Don't drop the "L-bomb" within the first several months.** You don't love him, you don't love the sex. On Fridays, you like the sport coat and like spending time with him. On Mondays, he's a "really fun guy" with nice eyes. (Good enough.) In the beginning, "I love you" is *way* too much information.

- **Don't use New Age words like *we, us, ours, destiny, soul mate*, or anything with a "togetherness" feeling.** Don't use catch phrases like *it was meant to be* or *the universe brought you to me*. Don't read him how the Sunday horoscope says your signs are compatible, and you are destined to be together. If he hasn't made up his mind yet, sappy words will scare the daylights out of him. Let him be the first to use those words with you. Then smile and say "Me too." Don't jump in his lap like you just won the Lotto.

- **Don't tell him about your therapy sessions, antidepressant drugs, or childhood issues.** And leave out the one about the bladder-control support group.

- **Don't try to be Mary Poppins or give him the "I'm trustworthy" speech.** Don't tell him you love charity work, orphans, and old people. Don't say, "I would never lie" (he'll think you told your first lie). Don't say that you would "never cheat" or that you "take commitment very seriously."

- **Don't try to rearrange his furniture to make your visits more tolerable.** He'll think you are moving in. Don't try to feng shui his place. Leave it the way you found it: "ghetto shui." The only way he'll get excited about feng shui is if he thinks it comes with free egg rolls and a fortune cookie. Instead, think like a bitch. Leave it nice and miserable at his place, so that when he visits your place it will feel like he's "Movin' on Up" like George and Weezy Jefferson.

- **Don't buy wife-like items such as towels or sheets.** If you buy a gift, get something less intimate, like a dog bed for his pet. Besides, when you do move in together, you'll want to liquidate all his crap at a garage sale anyway. That includes the junk his ex gave him. Plan it on the World Cup finals when his favorite team is playing. "See those huge boxes over there, sir? All that crap is one dollar. But only if you take everything before the game ends . . . ."

- **Don't introduce him as your boyfriend first. If he introduces you as his girlfriend, don't high-five the waitress, or gleefully do a victory dance like you just hit the motherlode.** Say nothing. Be cool. Act like it didn't register. If you are alone under the stars, and he says something like "I want you to be my girl"—remain cool as well. You can say something sweet and playful like, "Is that so?"

DESIRABILITY PRINCIPLE 27

The whole art of seduction involves the appearance of slight elusiveness.

This means don't answer all his unanswered questions about you. Don't be so blunt, obvious, or available that you come across as having already made up your mind about the guy.

Men *want* love and exclusivity just as much as women do. But he won't go there if it's expected or thrust upon him, *or if he didn't feel he had a choice in the matter.* The less you try to sell yourself, the more self-assured you'll seem. Just kick back, go out, and enjoy yourself. He'll come up with all of the above ideas. Your aura should say, "I believe in me." That breaks down in the male hard-wiring: *"She is secure within herself and knows how to handle a relationship."*

The reality is that men want "an emotional connection." One said, "A man wants all the things a woman wants. If you really care about her, you'll wonder what kind of wife she'd be. Men don't admit that because they don't want the woman knowing he cares *that* much. It's safer to express sexual interest only, because it's still considered 'manly.' But deep down, men want an emotional connection as well."

How to Keep Him Curious

Once you start getting cozy, avoid behaving in a way that allows him to predict your whereabouts at all times. He shouldn't feel that he can always reach you at the same time of day, each and every day. At night, he doesn't get a "round-the-clock booty calling card." If you had to wake up to answer his call, you are not to be joined twenty minutes later. If he texts you after midnight, you can respond sometimes, but other times wait until morning. Even during daylight hours, don't allow there to be an "electronic leash" around your neck with 24/7 access. If you always respond within 2 minutes to every text he sends, it will turn the relationship into a monotonous routine. He'll think, "Okay, I've got this one right where I want her. So let me put her on the backup reserve list and see who else is out there."

DESIRABILITY PRINCIPLE 28

You want to figure out his pattern, but don't let him figure out yours.

On the flip side, you don't want to make it seem like he is expected to check in, either. The mistake women often make is to try to keep tabs on the guy, which turns calling into a dreaded obligation. If he feels like his phone is a GPS tracking system that has been attached as an ankle device to assess his longitude and latitude at all times . . . congrats. His guard will go back up (and access to his heart will be denied).

He can't know you expect him to call or that your happiness depends on it. For example, Lauren was at home when Hugh called her, and they made small talk. Then he asked, "What are you doing for the rest of the evening?" Most women make the mistake of saying, "Oh, nothing. Just talking to you, sweetie." Then he thinks to himself, "Gee, doesn't take much to keep her happy." Instead, Lauren told him, "I'm taking a bubble bath, listening to a new CD, and then I'm watching a movie. I can't wait."

DESIRABILITY PRINCIPLE 29

Men are far more smitten when they feel like they are "stealing" your time away from something else you could have been doing.

It's not so much *how often* you call or whether you occasionally call him, but rather, *how your demeanor seems* when you talk to him. When he calls you . . .

1. ALWAYS ASK POSITIVE, HAPPY QUESTIONS LIKE:

"Hi, how was your day?" "How are you?"

This says: "Tell me something good, sugar pants."

It also tells him you want the tone of the relationship to remain positive, and you aren't a sponge for his negativity.

2. AVOID ASKING THINGS THAT SOUND LIKE A BOUNTY HUNTER CLOSING IN ON A FUGITIVE:

"Where did you go when you left work?"

"You didn't tell me where you were. I was worried."

"Why didn't you call?"

"Why didn't you text?"

"Your cell rang and went to voice mail. Why aren't you answering? Why is it on vibrate?"

This says: "Tell me something bad, you dirty, rotten scoundrel and lying SOB."

Negativity from you invites negativity from him.

Do you feel the difference? The second you shift into expecting a call or getting pissed when he doesn't call you, that's when he'll start to dodge you, or become more argumentative. If it goes on too long, the climate becomes hostile.

If you start out happy and upbeat, it sets the tone of the relationship. And, he'll keep dropping his guard until he gets deeply attached. The fact that you don't want to intrude will *draw him in a very, very big way*. At the onset, that's your *best* asset—more than sex, and more than beauty.

DESIRABILITY PRINCIPLE 30

When a woman makes a man feel he's trusted, it makes him feel strong and worthy. It makes him want to be honorable and do the right thing.

Deep down all men want to please their mommy. And when you are happy, he feels safe like he just brought home a good report card. Just like you want to feel secure, he wants to feel trusted. It makes him feel comforted and soothed: "This is not a waste of my time. I'm doing something right." It builds him up, and makes him feel like he doesn't want to break that trust. And, it makes him want to protect you even more.

The question women often ask is, "But what if I want him to call and text me more?" or, "What if I am upset because he didn't call me at a certain time?" Mia's situation provides a good example of how to effect a change in his behavior. She was used to hearing from John every night. He would get into his car after work at 5:00 and call her while he was stuck in traffic. She started to feel like he was "checking in," like she was just another errand. It became a little *too* convenient. But rather than ask him to make a change, she made a change. She simply stopped answering at 5:00.

If a man can normally reach you at 5:00 and then suddenly cannot, he'll call or text at 6:00 . . . at 7:00 . . . and at 8:00, or until he gets ahold of you. This is how you turn a boring phone call into an exciting event. Men love it when they are curious and they wonder and get all fired up about a woman. (And you mustn't deny him such a good time.)

If you agree to be somewhere or to call him at a certain time, it's very important to keep your word. It's the *random* phone calls you want to alternate. Here are a few more ways to get what you want, without having to nag or explain a word.

IF HE . . .	YOU SHOULD . . .
If he takes a few hours to return a phone call . . .	Take a few hours to pick up. Monkey see, monkey do. This will keep the relationship reciprocal and balanced.
If he keeps calling to push back the plans from 5:00 . . . to 6:00 . . . to 7:00 . . .	Agree to the first delay. If he pushes back again, pull the plug politely. Tell him to take care of his business and suggest hooking up later that week.
If he calls hours later than he said he was going to . . .	Let the answering machine pick up. It's amazing how quickly a couple of missed phone calls will make him ask, "Are you mad at me? I thought you were mad at me." (Correct answer: "Not at all. I've been crazy busy.")

If he calls at 9:00 and wants to get together at 10:00 . . .	Tell him you are going to bed early. That will make him plan his outings earlier, with more advance notice.
If he calls after 10:00 or at a time when you would normally be asleep . . .	Wait until your next date and politely tell him not to call you past 10:00. That shows you can live without talking to him, and you aren't that concerned with where he is at night.
If he wants to see you for one or two hours, or just enough time to have sex . . .	Tell him you don't work in "little time frames." Suggest another night when you both have more time.
If he doesn't call you when he's out of town . . .	He shouldn't be able to get ahold of you when he gets back.
If he is in a crabby mood and you aren't enjoying yourself . . .	Give him a kiss on the cheek, tell him you have an early morning, and go home.

Regardless of how many times a week he calls, texts, or wants to see you . . . don't be available 100 percent of the time. If you do, you will kill the chemistry.

DESIRABILITY PRINCIPLE 31

Men like rules and they like guidelines. If there's something you don't like, a quality guy will respect you for voicing your opinion. He wants to know what the "dos and don'ts" are.

It's actually a huge turn-on to most men when they are with a woman who behaves in a way that shows that she has a full life, and that if he wants to be in her world, he will have to integrate himself into *her* life.

This keeps a marriage spicy too. A girlfriend of mine, Nicole, recently got married to a European guy. Every year, he visits his parents in Europe. When I met her for lunch, she was on the cell phone telling her husband in Germany she was going to see a movie that evening. Then she ended the call and giggled. "He calls me three times a day to see what I'm up to. He wants to make sure I 'behave myself.'" Does she call him overseas? Nope.

Have you ever noticed that men love distracting you when you're on the phone? That's when they love kissing your neck or screwing up your concentration. There's nothing more interesting to a guy than a woman who is distracted or not focused on him.

Being unobtainable or independent is not just about distance or physical proximity. It has to do with how much of your mind space he has access to. You can be living separately and be totally *readable*, or you can be right in the next room and be very mysterious.

For example, Jenny lives with her boyfriend. She was complaining to him that she feels ignored when he watches TV on the couch. Then she did the opposite. She went into the bedroom and started reading a good book. After the third night, he turned the TV off early and climbed into bed, hoping to cuddle. She didn't immediately put the book down. Predictably, he started poking her, playfully hitting her, and acting like a little kid just to get attention from her.

DESIRABILITY PRINCIPLE 32

**Men love knowing there's a small part
of you that they can't get to.**

A married girlfriend of mine, Linda, said that whenever
her husband starts ignoring her, she'll go into the bathroom,
take out her makeup case, and start putting on her glamour-girl
face. Then she'll pick out a nice outfit and spray on some good
perfume. Instantly, her husband will become alarmed. "Where
are you going all dressed up?" So Linda will say something like,
"I'm going to Starbucks to meet Sue. We might go to that new
martini club," or, "I'm running some errands." And then he'll
ask her again, "You are going dressed . . . *like that*?"

Add to the equation that Linda's husband *knows* when
he's being neglectful. So immediately, he worries she might
want outside attention. And it never fails. Sometimes he'll
seduce her to keep her from going out, other times he'll have
dinner reservations or flowers when she gets back. How
many times have you decided to put on a little extra makeup
for no particular reason? It never fails. A male friend or business associate will ask, "You look nice. You got a hot date?"

DESIRABILITY PRINCIPLE 33

**Men read a lot into where you've been, by how dolled up
you are when you get home. If you are dolled up and you
weren't with him, it will keep him wondering a little.**

Sometimes women misinterpret the cliché "Men always want what they cannot have" and assume they have to have a rotation of guys coming around. So let's clarify. He doesn't have to compete with other men. He does have to "win" time from your other interests and all the little things that you like doing.

My girlfriend Helene is a real estate agent who recently got engaged. Her fiancé called and said, "Hey, meet me for happy hour." She told him she couldn't because she had to show a couple of properties at six o'clock. Then he tried to persuade her to cancel her appointments. "Oh, come on. It's happy hour!" And she jokingly quipped, "For me, happy hour is the hour after the check arrives in the mail. When I open up my envelope, I get happy for a whole hour."

DESIRABILITY PRINCIPLE 34

The second you put your life on hold, you become less interesting.

The thing to do is set the pattern from the beginning, when he's asking you out on dates. How? When you talk about when to get together, occasionally mention your *block out* times. In other words, the times he *can't* have access to you. This has to be done very subtly. Don't overdo it. But every now and then, throw in one of these.

BLOCK OUT TIMES

"I can't see you on _____ but I can see you on _____."

For example:

"I can't see you on Wednesday because I promised my girlfriend I'd go to her art opening. Want to do it Thursday?"

"I wish I could see you this weekend, that sounds fun. I have family visiting. Why don't we do it Tuesday night instead, after they leave?"

"This week I've got two deadlines at work. Can we get together this weekend?"

Don't do it to excess, and not all the time or he'll think it's a game, or you are reading a trashy relationship book about how to torture a guy (heaven forbid). So, be natural and authentic. Just don't give up all your other interests. Sometimes you are available, other times not, just like with any other friend.

If he sees he is not your only social outlet, he'll keep himself penciled into your schedule. And this has everything to do with marriage, because it demonstrates the most desirable characteristic he can have in a wife: You are whole within yourself, and you don't need him to validate your self-worth.

DESIRABILITY PRINCIPLE 35

The magic formula is to give a little time and energy to him . . . and then focus on your own life. Give a little . . . and then pull back.

It's a little like a schoolyard game of tag, and you are "it." If you stand there, he'll stop chasing you. But if you keep moving, he'll keep chasing after you. Even when you are married, it charges up his batteries whenever he can't have full access to you.

When Dolly Parton was asked the secret of being happily married for many decades, she said she just packs a bag and travels whenever her husband seems to be getting a little bit complacent. "That's my secret, honey . . . I just stay gone!"

3

THE SUN RISES AND SETS IN HIS

Boxer Shorts

How to Give Him Just the Right Amount of Spice in the Bedroom

*It's not premarital sex if you have
no intention of getting married.*

~GEORGE BURNS

Slow and Steady Wins the Race

Men often have a "Mary Ann vs. Ginger" debate about who was more desirable on *Gilligan's Island*. Ginger wore her sex appeal on her sleeve and flirted with everyone on the island. Most men would hump Ginger in the bushes, and not bother helping her out of the bushes when they were finished. On the flip side, most guys would pass on Ginger in a heartbeat if it meant having the chance to be with Mary Ann. Why? To most men, Mary Ann was more desirable sexually. She was wholesome. This made their imaginations run wild.

What does this have to do with marriage? For the Ginger type, he'll get a nice hotel room for the night. But for Mary Ann, he'll buy a million-dollar ranch on twelve acres of land, and put two BMWs in the garage. That's the girl he marries. Why? Men are territorial about their wives. With Mary Ann, he doesn't have to worry about her screwing the milkman while he's at work.

DESIRABILITY PRINCIPLE 36

Women are constantly being told amazing sex will win a man's heart. This is false. Just because a man sleeps with you doesn't mean he cares about you. Nor will good sex *make him care* about you.

Whom would you see a long-term future with? A Chippendale's dancer wearing a neon-yellow thong with singles inside his jockstrap, and plenty of wiggle in his jiggle? Or a nice-looking guy in a three-piece suit, with a 401(k)? Likewise, men want the whole package. They fantasize about having a quality woman they cuddle with next to a fireplace after sex. A quality guy usually won't stick around too long with a woman who publicly *cheapens* herself.

It's astonishing how often you see articles titled "100 Sex Tips That Will Drive Him Wild." Here's what these so-called experts *aren't sharing:* With adventurous sex that happens too quick and makes you seem like a seasoned pro, there won't be an emotional connection. Because of that, the sex will feel *ordinary to a guy.*

Let's say, hypothetically, that you followed all 100 suggestions. You busted out with the edible lingerie, the swing, the latex-related items, the bedroom acrobatics, and the furry handcuffs, and you had the disco ball twirling over the bed. Let's say you tied his hands and feet up with your stockings and got on all fours and barked like a dog. The million-dollar question is: Why doesn't it lead to long-term?

His first thought is:

"This is the best it's ever going to be."

His impression is:

"No challenge. Nothing else to work hard for."

His second thought is:

"The sex was automatic, and seemed almost routine. I wonder how many other guys she's done this with?"

Eventually he thinks:

"What I do will never be better than what she's already experienced. I am ordinary, therefore the sex is ordinary."

Every guy compares himself to other men. If he got you too easily, he assumes other men got you easily. And, every guy wants to delude himself into believing that he (in all his splendor) is going to be the one to introduce you to the wonderful world of sex. He'll be the one to teach you something new. And you have never had an orgasm before meeting him. If you did, he wants to believe it wasn't as good. So when you suggest positions he's never heard of, he knows you've already been "taught." Then he's thinking, "Why would I want to do tricks taught to her by some other guy?"

DESIRABILITY PRINCIPLE 37

When talking about quality men who are marriage material, a wholesome private "mine only" feeling is something men desire.

I recently spoke to an exotic dancer at a book signing. She told me that because of her career as an exotic dancer, she felt she had more "skills" to offer a prospective boyfriend. Two minutes later, she told me that she couldn't find a guy who would date her exclusively, and was meeting all the guys at work (while topless).

You don't need to enroll in an elite stripper academy and graduate with honors to figure out this riddle. First of all, women who work in the sex industry do not have a patent on pleasing a guy. Whatever they got . . . you got one too. That's first of all. Secondly, it does not require professional training or a degree in baton twirling. Pleasing a guy is very simple. (If he's not horny, make him a sandwich.)

Here's the part they didn't include in the curriculum at the elite stripper academy. Once a man categorizes you as having nothing else to contribute, you will be put in the "sex only" category. Once a woman is in the sex-only category, a guy won't have a commitment or relationship with her. Well, not exactly. In her mind it will seem like an evolving relationship. But in his mind? It's an ongoing one-night-stand that will last a few weeks or months.

Assuming a guy is not meeting a naked girl on a pole, a man will first assess any woman he meets by her clothing, or how she carries herself. Men look at how a woman dresses. Is she overplaying the sex card? A man named Doug explained, "It makes a woman *more* attractive if she's showing *less* skin. It makes you want to find out what's underneath."

If a woman wears something that doesn't "show all her business," like jeans, a heel, and a soft fuzzy sweater that shows her form, that's plenty. What a guy reads is:

"She seems well-rounded."

"It's not here on display for you."

"These are privileged areas."

"You'll have to work a little to get this."

. . . And just like that, her relationship potential and stock goes up.

You can be sexy, in a classy sexy way and that has a much more lasting impact. If she shows up wearing a rhinestone thong pulled up to her hips on the first date, or a miniskirt that could double as a tube top from the children's department, he will think the opposite:

"It's okay to play with the merchandise temporarily because it's on display."

"Any guy can get to it."

"I'm not special if I can get to her."

If a quality guy wants a serious relationship with a woman, he'd rather see less skin in public and keep the sex show private, for his eyes only. And he wants to unwrap the gift slowly.

This means cover up tattoos that are intended for private areas. Choose a clingy or formfitting blouse rather than a plunging neckline. Choose a sundress that shows a hint of silhouette. Or, a long skirt with a slit up the side over a micro-mini that shows the whole leg. Why? The peek-a-boo element. Not knowing when a leg will pop out triggers his imagination. And once you get him curious and *thinking about you*, that's when his thoughts turn to the future.

Playing Up the Feminine Card

When women look at clothing, we see colors, fabrics, and styles. What do men see?

1. Whether a woman is feminine and girlie.
2. Whether or not she is a mental challenge.
3. Whether she is confident.

If you want to make a man behave like a gentleman, play up your femininity. This will melt a guy every time. They have no defense for it.

Femininity to a guy is like kryptonite to Superman. The designer or brand name of your clothing isn't important to him. You will have more of an effect if you choose feminine fabrics, feminine colors, feminine items, and feminine makeup and scents.

Eric's experience is a good example of how quickly men categorize women. He met Jennifer through a work-related meeting. Eric asked her if she'd like to have drinks that evening after work. At the time, Jennifer was wearing a silk blouse and a pencil skirt, and a classic high heel. Before the date, Jennifer ran home to change into something she thought was "sexier." She put on a low cut blouse that showed a lot of cleavage, with jeans that sat very low on her hips. This showed off her new tattoo. She wore a cropped jean jacket that she took off. When she put it back on before leaving, he could see the lettering on the back which said, NOT EVERYTHING IS FLAT IN KANSAS.

Eric's take? "I liked the professional outfit much better, it was sexier." Most men with a J.O.B. think about how you will represent them if they are seen with you publicly at the annual Christmas party. More revealing does not equal more feminine. There's a reason they coined the phrase "feminine mystique." More mysterious and slightly less obvious . . . equals feminine. And, it also tells men that you are more confident.

DESIRABILITY PRINCIPLE 38

**When a man sees you wearing
very revealing clothes, he'll often assume
you don't have anything else going for you.**

. . . and he'll never take you seriously or think of you as having enough worth for a long-term relationship. Remember, when he sees you scantily dressed and exposed, he is not reminded of how great you look. He is reminded of other men you've slept with. But when he sees you wearing something feminine, he instantly feels more manly. This "mine only" feeling is more valuable than a sex costume or pole tricks.

In all the great love stories or movies, do you ever see a pole, a little-girl costume with polka dots, or a rubber number with buckles and dog collar? Absolutely not. That's what he wants from a prolonged one-night-stand with a woman he doesn't plan to permanently keep.

In fact, if a guy thinks you may be more seasoned sexually than he is, it automatically makes him think "short term" rather than long term. And most men find it a little emasculating. (That's when they start worrying whether they'll be the one wearing the polka-dot skirt in the family with polka-dot wedgies to match.)

DESIRABILITY PRINCIPLE 39

When you are playing for keeps, modest is hottest.

Why? When he's emotionally attached to a woman and wants to keep her around, he becomes a little insecure about how many other lovers she has had.

Think about it. If you buy a car that you intend to keep, naturally, you care about the mileage. Right? But if you rent one for the week or shorter term, the mileage really doesn't matter.

If a guy has feelings for you, it takes very little for their imaginations to run wild. For example, something as simple as the tattered condition of your undergarments gives him clues. If you go to his house and see female items in the bathroom, you might categorize him as a "player." With men it's the opposite. If he sees you wearing a sexy black panty and the elastic is a little frayed or tattered, he'll see it as evidence of a recent humping. The same goes for that black lacy see-through bra. If it's missing a hook or the hook is bent sideways (heaven forbid), he'll think it's been violently snatched off your body a time or two.

For this reason, hold fire on the five-piece triple XXX crotch-less outfit with fishnets, and fifteen straps, or the studded dog collar. It will have an "everybody's girlfriend" feel to it. Nor is it soft or feminine.

What most men said they find sexiest is a woman in one of his shirts with a sexy pair of panties underneath. This has a "mine only" feel. If you change into sleepwear, wear something silky that looks like you'd wear it for yourself when he's not around. (Translation: feminine.) This is more likely to make him appreciate the sex, and appreciate you also.

Stated or not, most guys want to feel like Farmer John plowing new terrain, and that no guy has travelled this terrain before. (Your job is to keep that illusion going.)

DESIRABILITY PRINCIPLE 40

If he is not willing to wait for sex, he is not worth your time. This is not a man who wants to be kept.

Exploring the Wonderland

Obviously, his objective at first is to jump into bed. Your objective is to preserve the possibility of long term, and take the long view . . . and that means there is no need to ride all the rides at Disneyland on your very first visit to the park.

On your first few dates, while your foot is on the brake and you are stalling the sex, he'll be breaking out all the stops. Since no man tells his tricks to a woman he's trying to seduce, I decided to fly below radar and find out the tricks men use. His first hurdle? To get past your front door at the end of the date.

HIS PLAYBOOK	YOUR PLAYBOOK
At the end of the night, he may ask, "Can I use your bathroom?"	Let him. Then wait with your winter coat and boots on and the umbrella still open. Don't take off one layer of clothing. Not even your gloves or hat.
He may do a few too many tequila shots and then say, "I'm too drunk to drive, can I sleep on your couch?"	He's hoping you'll say, "I'm not going to let you sleep on the couch, silly. You can sleep in my bed, but only if you behave." Instead, break out the strong Colombian coffee and call him a cab. He doesn't get past the kitchen.
He might offer a massage: "You've been under a lot of stress lately. How about I give you a back rub? I'll be a perfect gentleman, I promise."	After you get warmed up, he'll ask, "Could you unsnap your bra? I just want you to be more comfortable. Can you pull your shorts down to your ankles? I want to be able to massage your lower back. That's where your stress is . . . you poor thing."

HIS PLAYBOOK	YOUR PLAYBOOK
He might ask, "Can I come in for a second to use your phone? I need to check my voice mail and my cell phone went dead."	Let him use the phone. After that, be sure he "eases on down the road."
He may take the platonic approach: "Go change. Get comfortable. Pretend I'm not even here and do what you would ordinarily do if you were by yourself."	His first observation after you change will be, "Damn. She's not wearing a bra or underwear." Then he'll say, "Come lie down on the couch. Get a blanket. Let's just watch TV."
Last, but not least, is the cuddle trick. "I'll stay the night and we'll just cuddle as friends. I promise to leave my underwear on. Scout's honor." Then the story changes: "This underwear is way too constricting. It's itching me. I have to take them off. I hate when this happens . . . do you mind?"	(Game over.) Fast forward ten minutes. "I need to put it in just for a second. I want to know what it feels like to be inside you. We don't have to make love. Just the tip . . . I promise!" And the next thing you know, he's riding you like a Shetland pony.

The nice girl often gives in too early and then tries to do damage control. "I've never done this before. No, really. I don't usually do this with someone I barely know." When men hear this, they assume the opposite. They call it "the anti-slut defense."

Whenever you hear the words *don't worry* or *trust me*, be afraid . . . be very afraid. That's what the wolf said to Little Red Riding Hood. You should believe everything he says if you still believe in Santa Claus. Whenever a man says, "Don't worry, I promise that I will be a perfect gentleman," what he's saying is "I can't be trusted." If he's truly a gentleman, he doesn't need to announce it.

DESIRABILITY PRINCIPLE 41

The way to weed out a quality man from one that is not worthy of your time is his patience about waiting to have sex. If he likes you, he'll be happy just being in your company.

If he's going to leave you because you won't sleep with you fast enough, he would have left after getting it also.

To all guys, sex is like his favorite spectator sport: football. He will try to "move the ball" down the field a few yards at a time. Then he gets a new line of scrimmage, a first down, and another opportunity to score. If he struggles, his love of the game is elevated. "Woo-hoo!" Butts get spanked and champagne bottles get popped. *He secretly wants you to give him some resistance.* Because if you just give him the ball and an empty field . . . all the stimulation will be taken out of it.

Paige didn't realize this when she tried to seduce Ted. They had gone out twice but hadn't been intimate. On their third date, they were leaving for dinner when she said, "I went shopping and I want to show you what I bought." Then she pulled out whipped cream and a G-string made out of red licorice. "I hope you like strawberry because we are going to try this stuff out later tonight." Paige thought that Ted would fall out of his tree. "I'll get him so turned him on, he'll never be able to resist me. Then he'll marry me." Instead, it did the opposite: *It accelerated the rate at which he grew tired of her.*

The first way to discern if he's truly interested in you is to take note of how you are spending your time outside the bedroom. Does he spend time with you during the daylight hours? Is he interested in what you like? This is very telling. Even if you like doing something a little boring, like taking your dog to the park, a guy who is really into you will be excited to come along anyway. Silly things will be interesting to him because they are something that you are into, and he finds *you* exciting.

DESIRABILITY PRINCIPLE 42

If you appear cautious, that will come across to a quality guy as though you have high self-worth.

Laurie is a perfect example of this. She lives in NYC and Sean commuted to Long Island. After two dinners together, he called her and asked, "Could I sleep on your couch tonight? I have an early morning tomorrow in the city. That way we could go to dinner and I could be a block away from my appointment." Laurie told him she wasn't feeling up to it, and she didn't have to explain why. He got it. And it instantly raised her desirability in his eyes.

The following suggestions will set a classy tone, so he views you as someone he can take seriously.

- **Don't talk about places you'd like to have sex or what your favorite humping music is.** He doesn't marry the girl who tells him, in the first phone conversation, she likes being "spanked by Daddy" with a broken car antenna in the backseat of the car.

- **Plan activities.** Don't start the dating pattern of hanging out and watching videos. Not unless you want dinner reservations to sound like this: "We'll have two cheeseburgers, a large fries, and some Tater Tots. I'll drive around and pick that up at the second window."

- **Dress a little sexy, but not too revealingly.** When you show a little but not everything, his read is, "Now that's a woman who is in control." Remember, modest is hottest.

- **Avoid heavy petting on the couch or bed until you are 100 percent ready to go the distance.** It's always safe to kiss while standing *vertically* in a door or lobby. There's a reason that they call it the "horizontal mambo."

- **Invite him in *before* you leave for your dinner date.** Let him pick you up at six thirty if the reservations are for seven thirty. Have a glass of wine and let him meet the cat or the dog. This helps break the ice, and prevents late-night access. Then when you send him on his way at the end of the date, it won't seem so impersonal.

- **No crying in your beer about how the ex did you wrong.** Don't say he was a jerk, that he drove too fast, or that he spent all your money. All that does is reduce your worth in his eyes. Leave the "poor me" story out of the conversation. Besides, it's none of his business. If he asks about the ex, simply say, "Long and boring story. [*Yawn.*]" Translation: "Over it."

- **When the kissing starts getting heated and you want to stop, don't say "quit it" or "stop it" or "knock it off" like a whiny young girl.** The *key is to stop him with your body language.* If his hand is trying to do meet-and-greet with your derriere, this is a good time to reach back there and hold that friendly little hand, and then gently ease away. "We'll miss the show if we don't get going." This also exudes that you are a woman in control. Now he is forced to feel respect for you.

It's best to avoid heavy petting on the couch for another reason: If you bring him to the point of no return and then hit the kill switch at the last minute, he'll resent it. Besides, you won't sound too convincing if you say, "Not yet, I want it to be special." Especially if you've been dry humping him for an hour and your hand is keeping it warm in his boxers when you break the news. It's a little too late to stop the fiesta when his tool is doing the cha-cha, and the "Boot Scootin' Boogie" in his britches.

DESIRABILITY PRINCIPLE 43

The purpose of waiting is not just to seem classier. You also want to give yourself time to find out certain important facts about him.

. . . like whether he has a wife and three kids in another state. Or whether all his friends are hoodlums. You want to figure out whether the ex-girlfriend is still having "breakup sex" with him (because she doesn't know they've broken up yet). You want to know if he's 38 and still lives at home. You want to figure out if he has three DUIs or a crack habit. And you want to find out about his college days and whether he went roller-blading through the streets of San Francisco wearing Daisy Dukes and a leotard.

Time allows you to smoke him out. See who he is. And don't adopt the philosophy of Sir Isaac Newton, who said, "What goes up must come down." Don't apply that rule to sex. Remember the sign you see when you walk into a place of business: "We reserve the right to refuse service to anyone"? Hang that one on your bedroom door.

You Should Refuse If:

IF HE IS TOO AGGRESSIVE

If he's interested in you, he won't be too grabby or proposition you on the first couple of dates because he won't want you to think he's a pig. If sex is all he's focused on, that demonstrates going in that he's not concerned with who you are. If a little resistance is too much for the guy and he takes off, you are better off. In fact, clear a path for him and make sure there's nothing in his way on the way out.

IF HE WON'T STAY THE NIGHT

Don't sleep with a guy who tells you, "I can't stay the night," or a guy who tells you that you can't stay at his place. This guy is already warning you before you have sex that he intends to keep you at arm's length. If you are making out and he says, "I can't stay over," that's your cue to say, "Who said you were staying over?"

IF THERE ARE TOO MANY "QUEENS IN THE CASTLE"

Don't get sexually involved with him if he makes it obvious he has a harem of female "friends" waiting to come in off the wings and take your place. And it doesn't matter if he swears they are "just friends." Listen to your gut.

IF YOU DON'T FEEL COMFORTABLE

Your instincts are the most valuable thing you have. Never, ever allow anyone to talk you out of what you feel. As Kim Basinger said: "I feel there are two people inside me—me and my intuition. If I go against her, she'll screw me every time, and if I follow her, we get along quite nicely." Nothing is more important than your body and your health. Treat them like they have some worth.

The nice girl knows that certain guys are "hit and run" artists, but they get seduced by the naughty-girl element. Before long, she starts convincing herself there is a potential for a relationship. "It will be different with me! I will be the one to reform this guy. I can change him."

For example, he'll be on the bed with a woman making all the moves. Then she'll stop and say, "Wait. I feel like things are moving too fast. I barely know you." So the guy lies back on the bed and says, "Okay, ask me anything you want to know, and I'll tell you. I am an open book." (It's like a sales negotiation. Find out what the objection is and then overcome the objection.) So he tells her a sob story about how his first love broke his heart, and how *used* he felt. Then he shows her the scar on his leg, or how his parents liked his older brother better. Then he touches her cheek gently like he's Fabio. "We don't have to have sex if you aren't ready," he says (while he's thinking, "What other B.S. can I come up with to get her in the sack?"). What does she say? "I am ready! I am yours!" And next thing you know, the downstairs neighbors have plaster falling down off their ceiling until 2:00 A.M.

Fast forward one week for a "state of the union" address. "I don't know why he's not calling. He said we had a connection. It was emotional. He said it wasn't sex . . . it was making love. He said I was special. Maybe we just got off on the wrong foot. Maybe we're just going through a little rough patch in our relationship."

DESIRABILITY PRINCIPLE 44

**Who he *tells* you he is in the beginning
has very little to do with how he will *treat* you.
If there's sex involved, he'll promise
you things you've never even heard of.**

Dating websites are notoriously misleading for this reason. When a guy is asked to check the box to indicate what type of match he's looking for, which one do you think he's going to check if he just wants sex?

- Casual sex with no protection, and no phone call the next day.
- Commitment, love, and poems under a tree.

He'll check the one that says "commitment." Because he is very committed (to seeing you naked).

After all, men are hunters. We're dealing with a red-blooded hunting creature that prides himself on his ability to conquer. If it were legal, men would have their ex-conquests' heads mounted on the wall, in the den. A bighorn sheep . . . a moose . . . a ten-point deer . . . Jennifer . . . Natalie . . . and a fling named Vanessa (because one-night stands get mounted too).

The actor Vince Vaughn is quoted as saying, "If I'm not interested in a woman, I'm straightforward. Right after sex, I usually say, 'I can't do this anymore. Thanks for coming over!'" No guy is going to say, "I would never marry you. But I really want to get laid." If he's not sincerely interested in you, it's not uncommon for him to say what you want to hear. "Marriage? Kids? A big house? I can hardly wait." Whichever ear it hits first, make sure it flows all the way through and makes its way out the other ear.

Women who are on dating websites should reconsider the language. Make sure you don't appear to be in love with a fantasy. It doesn't make a guy feel "special" if a woman advertises she is looking for "Sunsets, romance, and wine and cheese on the beach" with any chump. He wants a woman who is receptive to him, not everyone else. If some creepy guy that looks like he'd be suspected of killing Kennedy responds to her dating profile and promises her the moon, he doesn't want her to break out the chocolate-covered strawberries.

As the "huntee," the intelligent choice for you is not to roll around on the bed or couch until you really get to know the guy. Wait until you feel comfortable. Give him some time to *show* you—not just *tell* you—who he is with his *actions*.

Dinners, flowers, and being a gentleman—these are the basics if he sees you as the girl of his dreams.

Keeping the Home Fires Burning

When you become lovers, it's still important to understand that men are evaluating the long-term potential of the relationship. They don't need a woman with exceptional skills.

DESIRABILITY PRINCIPLE 45

What most men are looking for is a woman who is natural in bed and who genuinely enjoys sex with him.

So I asked men, "What are the clues that a woman isn't into it?" Here is some of the feedback they gave:

Clues You Aren't Really Into the Sex

- John said, "A lot of women scream in a pitch that would stop a charging rhino dead in its tracks. They flip their hair around, strike exotic poses, and put on a stage performance. It's like they think they are being videotaped and there's a professional film crew in the room. Lights . . . camera . . . action!"
- Marcus said, "Try not to make it obvious you're watching the clock or keeping track of time. Before sex, don't say, 'It's eight forty-five. We have to stop in fifteen minutes, because my favorite cooking show starts at nine o'clock.'"
- Kent said, "Most guys would much rather have an attractive woman who is really into the sex than a supermodel who isn't really into it. Hands down."
- Frank said, "You know the woman is not all there when she's screaming and hyperventilating, and you haven't even put it in yet. So I'll stop what I'm doing to see what kind of noises she's going to make. If she's screaming and I'm not even touching her, I feel like I can go grab a sandwich and then come back and pick up where I left off."

Men tend to assume that the theatrical performance has nothing to do with their performance. He'll think, "Well, I see she's not into me." And as soon as he gets the vibe you are *not* enjoying the sex, it will be a deal breaker in regard to commitment.

There's no panel of judges giving you a score: "I give a 9.0 for artistic showmanship but a 7.8 for technical performance." If he makes you feel that way, that means he's a lousy lover—not you. With a good lover, you don't worry about whether you need a boob job or whether he can see the cellulite on your left butt cheek, because the guy has you sufficiently distracted.

Don't ever point out a physical flaw to a man (real or imagined). That includes inside and outside the bedroom. Don't tell him what you used to look like. Or what you used to weigh. Don't point to a chipped tooth, and tell him how you want veneers. Save all your consultations regarding a facelift or liposuction for the doctor's office.

DESIRABILITY PRINCIPLE 46

Men I spoke with said that they rarely pay attention to a woman's flaws until she points them out to him.

They find the female form beautiful, and they are admiring what's right. So when he runs his hand across your stomach and you say, "I'm doing crunches and it will be flat by summer," he assumes you are busy scrutinizing your own body, and not thinking about his.

According to men, another mistake women make is that they try to act prim and proper, and virginal. This makes men suspicious. He's no altar boy, and he knows you are no virgin. You'll seem classier if you say nothing about your previous lovers. Besides, even a third-grader can do the math. (Mr. Rogers music.) "Good morning, boys and girls. Today we have a word problem. If the ratio of men to women is equal, and all the men have had sex with dozens of women, is it mathematically possible that all women have had sex with only three men? The child who cracks this unsolved mystery will win a gold star and a cap with a propeller on top."

The way men infer that you are loose is not by what you say. They judge by how sophisticated your technique is the first time you are intimate. If you want him to see you as his long-term love, you can't make it seem like half the animals of Noah's Ark have been inside your bed. Don't try to come across as the expert humping champion.

It's like . . . a tomato.

No one wants to take home the tomato at the market that everyone else squeezed. (But if he doesn't know everybody squeezed it, he'll buy it and bring it home.)

Rest assured, he'll pick up on any little sign that you've recently returned from a humping spree. Hence the need for us to take a tour of your place to make sure you seem like a classy woman. A hot tomato that has few squeezes. Think of it as . . . the sexual innocence project.

THE SEXUAL INNOCENCE PROJECT

- The first time you have sex, don't recycle previously worn hoochie gear. Wear that stuff later on, and make sure he sees you take it out of the bag with the price tags still attached. (I'm serious. Save the bag.) Until then, a pretty lace bra-and-panty set under your clothes is fine. Don't bolt into the bathroom and change into a Madonna corset with a lime-green thong and a studded dog collar. It will seem too rehearsed, and *too* premeditated.

- Never open a drawer where you keep exotic novelties, like a battery operated turbo toy. If it's bigger than a baseball bat and comes with a clutch and a gear shift, it will ruin the warm and fuzzy ambience. After all, you don't want him feeling like a puddle-jumping Cessna airplane parked next to a 747 jumbo-jet.

- Let him suggest the sexual positions the first couple of times. If you break out sexual acrobatics (that have him saying "ouch") and commence to steady riding *him* like a cowboy, he'll think, "This one has been to a few rodeos."

- Don't be in a mad rush to fling your clothes off in every direction and jump right into mounting position like a cat in heat. Let him be the one to undress you . . . *slowly*. It will keep you from looking like a seasoned pro.

- Let him supply the condom. And whatever you do, don't do any tricks where you put the condom in your mouth and then seductively put it on his private parts. "Look at me, Mom! No hands!" He'll think you enrolled and got your "ho" certification. That will guarantee that he'll classify you as short-term. Act like you wouldn't even know where to buy a condom much less identify what one looks like.

- If he didn't bring a condom, never let him see where you hide yours. He can't see the Value Pack from Costco that started out with five hundred condoms (and is now 75 percent empty). Even if it's a twelve-pack and there are six missing, that's six times someone else was inside you. (Not exactly a "mine only" ambience.)

- If he complains about wearing a condom, never say, "*All my boyfriends* wear them and I never have sex without one." If you have a child, don't say, "You have to wear one because I get pregnant really easily." (That will serve to clarify why the Value Pack is now 75 percent empty.)

- Remember, men like women who are girlie. They love lightly scented lotions and anything soft and feminine. (If he sees you have a restraint system on the bed, it might concern him a bit.)

- All men are very insecure about their size. If he's not gifted, you can't look at it and blurt out, "Is that all?" It's in the fine print of your contract. You are required to say, "Ooh. Oh boy. I just can't handle all that. Easy, easy. You are going to knock my back out of alignment."

- The first time he stays over, don't look like you were too prepared with the overnight kit, or that you are *used to* male sleepovers. Don't put out extra boxers, a razor, and a toothbrush. Also, don't leave the Petco products in the shower. If the other stuff is strawberry scented, he'll use the flea-and-tick shampoo by mistake.

- Don't serve a five-course breakfast in bed. If you own a magazine that has a picture in it with a breakfast tray, poached eggs, and lilies from the garden—throw it out as a preventative measure so you don't get any bright ideas. Instead, direct him to the nearest coffee shop and ask him to bring you back a cafe latte. And a pretty cookie.

- During pillow talk don't whisper in his ear, "You complete me," or, "I always knew we'd be together." He shouldn't feel he was seduced by *you*. He wants to feel he did the conquering, not the other way around.

Several men also said that they like input from a woman in bed. However, they don't want you to give them a report card or a play-by-play the next day. You can't do the Monday morning postgame review with a pointer in your hand, and a huge chalkboard on the wall, like the guy is retarded. "This is your position X . . . *here*. This is the hopeful O. *That's me*. When I call the play, your objective will be to run, find the hole, and focus on the G-spot."

For all ego-intensive purposes, any Monday-morning quarterbacking will crush him. Show him or tell him what you want *during* the act . . . or forever hold your peace. Tact is important, especially when dealing with his performance and his "best friend."

WARNING TO MEN:
Skip the next paragraph.
Reading it may cause nightmares.

Bobby told me a story about Charlene, who committed a cardinal no-no with the male privates. Charlene was lying on the bed enjoying the afterglow of sex. Bobby had gotten up and was getting dressed. As he bent over to pick up his socks he put one leg up on a chair. Charlene thought his "little trinkets" looked cute and thumped them from behind to see if they would swing. As his knees buckled, he began to hyperventilate and see stars. Psychic hotline prediction: If you do this, you will not hear wedding bells, because he will disappear and stay gone forever. (Nor will he remember you with great fondness and nostalgia.) After he gets treatment for his post-traumatic stress disorder, it is highly unlikely you will ever hear from him again.

With respect to pillow talk, silence is golden. Don't ask questions like "Was it special? Do you love me? Was it good? How good? Better than that other girl? The best you ever had?" If the first thing he hears after sex is "That was so much better than that other guy . . . he was a two-pump chump with thirty seconds of fury," he'll feel like one of many. He doesn't want to picture you with any other guy, so it's always best not to bring up other men. Don't make any sexual comparisons—good or bad.

Also, don't believe what he says when he professes his love to you right after sex. If he starts talking about "the future," what he really means is the sex was really good . . . and he wants to try a different position (in the future).

Keeping the Mental Challenge After Sex

Women are told that as long as they wait out the five-date rule or the requisite one-month time period before having sex, a man will automatically commit and the "deal has been sealed." She's thinking, "All the games are over. I've reached the goal line. We are now a couple." Right? Don't run out and buy matching "his and hers" terry-cloth bathrobes just yet. You are only at halftime, sister.

Let's rewind. You got down; it wasn't too bad. And now he thinks he's Joe Stud in the bedroom. The morning after, he's cockier than a peacock in prime mating season. He's singing "We Are the Champions" in the shower. "She left walking with a limp. Her legs are probably still quivering. She'll never be able to *think* about sex again without envisioning my face with a halo around it." In his mind, you've been intimate so he thinks he has all the power. (That's about to change.)

When I interviewed men, I posed the following question: "What would happen if a woman just behaved no differently after sex? What if she was pleasant, but went on about her business like nothing had changed?" (I wish I could videotape their reactions and play them back for you.) Some men turned white. One guy said, "That would turn my world upside down." Most admitted it would freak them out. (Good to know.)

To better understand the "his and hers" dynamics of what's going on immediately after sex, let's review a play-by-play.

WHAT HE FIRST ANTICIPATES AFTER SEX

He's been through the drill with other women and knows that after sex you are likely to expect boyfriendlike behaviors. He will pull back simply because he thinks that a lot will be expected of him. Act like you expect absolutely nothing. Don't be more, or less, affectionate. Act no differently. Be the same girl. Here's why that will work to your advantage.

WHY HE'LL PULL BACK

Men want to postpone commitment. He'll alter the dating pattern to avoid regularity and consistency. Why? Because to him, regularity + continuity = commitment. This is why he may pull back, make the rules, break them, switch the rules, and then do another changeup. He'll call more randomly. He'll try to see you on short notice. And he'll try to keep you in second-guessing mode.

HOW HE THINKS YOU'LL RESPOND TO HIS PULLING BACK

He's expecting you to be available 100 percent of the time. When you push, or if you are doting, clingy, or want time and reassurance right after the first time you have sex, he will think that pulling back and keeping you at arm's length is justified. And then he'll make himself scarce.

WHAT YOU SHOULD DO

Do the opposite. Stay on the go. Don't pick up the phone all the time. If he calls and you are busy, tell him you will call him back. Stay busy with your own life. Don't be available at the last minute or seem ready to go anytime he wants to see you.

WHAT MESSAGE THIS SENDS

You won't be doing all the heavy lifting in the relationship. Now it becomes a relationship of value to him because he sees that you aren't willing to jump into something and give yourself away, just because of one night of passion. Now he sees you as a cool person, not an insecure woman making demands.

WHY THIS LEADS TO COMMITMENT

He'll think, "If she's not freaking out, I guess things weren't progressing as fast as I thought they were." Then he'll revert to his original routine and continue to pursue you.

WHY THIS IS THE ULTIMATE COUP DE GRÂCE

It's a mild ego blow. Now you have his full attention. He's thinking, "That's odd, I thought I was Mack Daddy in the sheets. My phone should be ringing off the hook. What's going on here? Why isn't she chasing me like all the rest of them?"

If a guy doesn't call you after he's been having crazy sex with you, it's because he is expecting a needy reaction. He's fearing intensity and neediness. Getting the opposite will throw him for a loop and change his orientation very quickly. Now he realizes you are stronger than the rest: "She has standards. She is not a weakling. She is not giggly, stupid, or naïve. She's nobody's pushover."

DESIRABILITY PRINCIPLE 47

A woman who behaves more coolly and casually after sex *is the exact opposite* of what he is used to experiencing.

He'll also wonder why you aren't asking the typical questions he's used to hearing:

- Are we exclusive?
- Are we still cool?
- What's wrong?
- Why do you seem so distant?
- Are you mad at me?
- Is everything okay?

You want him to ask these questions of you. When you don't become needy, he'll become fixated on why you *aren't* fixated. "Wait a minute. Why isn't she screaming or asking me where I've been? Maybe she was holding back. Maybe it takes more to impress this one. I better step up my game."

DESIRABILITY PRINCIPLE 48

When you aren't mind-blown after sex, and you continue to focus on your own life, he'll start looking at you differently. Then he'll start wanting to secure a relationship with you.

It's like child-rearing. During the first year, psychologists say, you should "enthrone" the toddler. After one year, you are supposed to dethrone the toddler to keep him or her from having a really bad case of the "terrible twos." The same can be applied to men. After sex, you have to make sure that he doesn't think he's the only one running the show. If he does, chances are you won't be headed toward a commitment.

A lot of women think that the way to reduce themselves to a booty call is to sleep with a guy too soon. But it really has more to do with *how available she is after sex*. She's thinking that after sex, she's died and gone to heaven. She's expecting Hallmark cards, poems under a tree, and walks on the beach. She gets her hair done for him, dresses for him, and even suffers third-degree burns from her bikini wax to have a pretty "poodle clip" for him. That's when a woman is most likely to be at a man's beck and call. He says, "Baby, I miss you. Can I come over?" (Translation: "I'm horny.") She thinks, "He's my boyfriend now, so what's the harm?" Here's the harm: You are relaxing the standards. And if you do it once or twice? Congrats. You've just set a late-night pattern of being his sex-buddy.

DESIRABILITY PRINCIPLE 49
After sex, behave as if the relationship is still new.

Men respect anything that they have to invest effort into. It's no different than a teenager with a new sports car. If you hand the keys to an expensive luxury convertible to a sixteen-year-old on a silver platter, he'll get into all kinds of trouble. He'll get speeding tickets, he'll bang it up, and he won't take care of it. But if the same kid has to go out and mow some lawns, trim some trees, and flip a few burgers over the summer, he'll be much more protective of that car. If a buddy of his says, "Hey, let's burn some rubber and see how fast this will go," he'll say, "Are you crazy? I worked all summer to buy these tires."

Michael told a very simple yet poignant story about how his fiancée, Kate, won his respect because she kept her presence of mind after sex. The first weekend they were intimate, Kate got a call from her aunt on Sunday morning from South America. She told Michael that it might take a while. Five minutes passed before he started clearing his throat to hint that he wanted her to get off the phone. Kate covered the receiver and whispered, "Do you have something else you need to take care of? Please don't let me keep you if you need to go."

Certainly not the advice one might anticipate reading in a Miss Manners column, which would probably advise you to say, "How rude of me. I will jump off the phone and fetch your slippers too!" Kate gave Michael the vibe that said he was free to go—in stark contrast to most women, who typically dote on the guy. What it showed was: "I'm not going to stop being who I've always been because of a night of passion. This is my world and I'm not going to stop living the way I always have."

DESIRABILITY PRINCIPLE 50

Men are intrigued by anything they do not completely control.

And when you are upset or sprung, he knows he's in control. So cool your jets. Chill. After sex, just do what guys do: Make a sandwich. Watch a little ESPN. Order Pay Per View wrestling. Watch *SportsCenter*. And then fall asleep on the couch, in that worn-in spot with the butt imprint on it.

Don't agree to let him stop by without calling. Let him put forth some effort. If you pick him up at the airport at midnight, drop him off at his place and split. Regardless of the reason, don't be a late-night convenience. In the South, they have the slang phrase *go stupid*. After sex, don't go stupid on him. Make him treat you with respect.

Don't assume, "That's how guys are. They don't plan things in advance. They don't go out of their way." Wrong. Does he miss the kickoff at the Super Bowl? Absolutely not. If something is important, it gets priority. On the big game day, he'll be checking the batteries in the remote, making sure the beers are on ice, and warming up that favorite worn-in spot on the couch . . . two hours before the coin toss.

When you don't chase him, he'll come looking for "his girl." Dana and Adam are the perfect story of how a man will come and track you down. They had just slept together and Adam told her he was splitting town with the boys. "I'm going away. [Then he eyed her expecting a response.] Do you have any feelings on this?" He expected her to flip out and reassured her that his cell phone would be on all weekend, but she didn't call. That Saturday night, she went out with the girls. When she came in, there were nine missed calls and four voice mails. (Notice: It doesn't matter how busy he is. If he wants to reach you, he'll find time to call.) The following morning, Dana returned home from church to find Adam sitting outside on the front steps of her apartment. The second he can't get ahold of you he'll send out an APB, or an "all points bulletin," to find you.

DESIRABILITY PRINCIPLE 51

When you maintain a bit of privacy and he has to wonder a little where you are, it stimulates his imagination.

Jacqueline Kennedy Onassis said, "There are two types of women: those who want power in the world, and those who want power in bed." And there's a third type: the bitch. She gets both.

The Thrill of Victory

Picture a guy walking by the water cooler at work. He overhears two secretaries talking and one says, "I'm not giving him any." Instantly, his ears perk up and it gets stored in his memory bank. There are certain attitudes women have toward sex that register with a man. Here's why the whole idea of "giving him some" doesn't go over well. If he's a good lover, he wants to believe that he's giving you as much pleasure as you are giving him. And that his "somethin' somethin'" is hard to resist.

That said, there are times you don't want to have sex. After all, women just aren't as physically strong. We can't lift a heavy box like they can, we can't open a jar—and sometimes we just don't have the physical fortitude to be a pin cushion after a long hard day of chasing kids or meeting work deadlines. If you explain it to him, be sure to do it in a way that makes him feel big and strong while presenting yourself as the delicate little flower. This way you can negotiate a foot massage or a shoulder massage and avoid making him feel rejected. If he feels rejected on an ongoing basis, he will eventually disconnect from the relationship.

DESIRABILITY PRINCIPLE 52

To a man, a long term relationship with long periods of no sex represents a relationship with no love, no affection, and no emotional connection.

Since most women don't have the same sex drive as men, the frequency of sex often becomes an issue. The way to avert this is to keep him surprised sexually. Then he gets physical and mental stimulation, and is a little off balance. When a man can anticipate that he will have sex twice a week at a particular time and in a particular position, he'll begin to feel resentful, as though he's been put on a sexual Slim-Fast diet. But when you keep him surprised, he's always flashing back to the images of hot moments you've recently shared.

DESIRABILITY PRINCIPLE 53

Always preserve the mystery.
Keep your sex sporadic and unpredictable.
It makes it much more intense for a man.

Now, instead of the predictable "turkey tidbits on Thursdays," he feels like he is never too far from an all-you-can-eat buffet. If you have sex in the hallway on Tuesday and surprise him in the laundry room on Friday—the memories will be burned in his mind. Guys don't forget stuff like that. Now the *mental foreplay* is ongoing 24/7—even though you may still only be having sex twice a week.

Never underestimate the power of what you say to a man, before or after sex. A man will put far more value in a relationship and feel more connected to you when you genuinely enjoy the sex and make him feel his "stuff" is extra-special. If you crush his ego, "big daddy" will quickly become "crabby daddy." And then he'll want no part of a commitment.

After all, the way to his heart isn't through his stomach . . . it's through his boxer shorts.

4

Female Button Pushing:

A TIME-HONORED MALE TRADITION

Why Men Deliberately Annoy Women to Figure Out Where They Stand

Well, you know, boys. A nuclear reactor is a lot like women. You just have to read the manual and press the right button.

~HOMER SIMPSON, ON *THE SIMPSONS*

Taking Control of Your Emotions

If you were a fly on the wall listening to a group of men talking, it wouldn't be uncommon to hear them discuss how men are "logical" and women are loose cannons with no emotional control. Like apple pie and baseball, commiserating with his peers ranks among his all-time favorite pastimes. Drinking . . . golfing . . . hunting . . . fishing . . . and some good old-fashioned female-story swapping.

This is why men love the Jack Nicholson line from the movie *As Good As It Gets.* When Nicholson's character is asked how he can write a woman's temperament so well, he responds, "I think of a man. Then I take away all reason and accountability." This is how many men perceive women.

Now comes the dirty little secret they don't want you knowing about: A guy will annoy you deliberately, egg you on, and then be alert to your response. He'll consciously probe around the edges of your "nice girl" façade to see what he will be dealing with. He wants to know what your backbone is like. He wants to see how alert and smart you are. He wants to see if you recognize when he behaves poorly.

No guy will come in at the end of a bad day and say, "Honey, I need spooning and cuddle time." Instead, he may try to get attention by provoking you. Then he figures out where he stands by how emotional you become. When you are upset he knows you care and he knows he's in control.

DESIRABILITY PRINCIPLE 54

When a woman reacts emotionally, men get three things: attention, control, and the feeling of importance.

In the real world, relationships don't exactly go down like a G-rated plot about sunshine and puppy dogs. Whereas women see no logic in purposefully pissing someone off, men see testing as a tool. I affectionately refer to this process as a "testofest."

 Testofest

A strategic, premeditated dating ritual that involves pushing your buttons. The test usually begins with his pulling back in some way just to see what will happen. He may deliberately forget to call. He may look at another woman. In each instance, he's evaluating your response. He's expecting an involuntary reflex caused by a lack of emotional self-control.

After all, relationships don't always come in neat little packages. And sometimes a man will push your pressure points just to see how you react. The second he sees super-charged emotions that he thinks are disproportionate to the perceived snub, you'll quickly get categorized as a woman who can't be taken too seriously. If your feet stomp, tears squirt across the room, and you start screaming in a pitch that would stop a charging rhino, *he will know how much power he has over you*. And:

DESIRABILITY PRINCIPLE 55

When you are easily manipulated, he will assume he doesn't have to give as much in the way of a commitment in order to keep you there.

If, on the other hand, you don't become unhinged and you respond with a level head, he'll see it as a sign of strength. His trust and respect will deepen, and he'll want to take the relationship to the next level. Instantly, he'll shift gears because he'll realize he's dealing with *an equal*.

For example, let's say a guy comes home after a really rough day at the job. He won't say, "Darling, I need attention." Instead, he'll get into a verbal skirmish with you. And, he gets the feeling of satisfaction after you kiss and make up. This encourages him to use you as an emotional punching bag. On the other hand, you can give him no reward. Say, "Okay. I can see you've had a crummy day.

I'll let you wind down and I'll be back in an hour. I'll put a beer in the freezer for you. By the time you get out of the shower it will be really cold. See you later." Then split, and stay gone for two hours. Then you will have his full respect. Why? He's thinking, "That was smooth. She saw it coming and read me like an open book. Hmm . . . she sure sidestepped that. I guess being a jerk will get me replaced."

DESIRABILITY PRINCIPLE 56

An emotional reaction is always a reward, even if it's negative attention.

Therefore, the best way to set limits with a guy who is testing you is by controlling the ebb and flow of your attention. In his mind, he doesn't think he's being a jerk, because he has a specific purpose. So he probes around the edges to find out:

- What are the important things about her that I don't know about yet?

- What will she be like when she's at her worst, or when she feels wronged?

It's a cross between a "gotcha" game and Pop Goes the Weasel. (Hint: you are the weasel.) He's looking to see if you'll be able to hold your own or whether you will fall apart like a five-year-old having a tantrum at Toys "R" Us.

Remember, there is a fine line between testing and disrespect. So let's do a quick side-by-side comparison.

A TEST	VERSUS DISRESPECT
Usually early on after sex, he will pull back to see how you'll react.	Disrespect is repeated and continual. His inattention is more blatant, more mean-spirited, and usually a sign that the relationship has eroded over a period of time.
He'll call and cancel a date, just to see how you respond and whether you'll be flexible.	He won't call. He'll just stand you up and call a day or two later with a really elaborate half-baked story.
He'll glance at another woman to see how you react, hoping you'll cling to him more tightly.	He'll talk to another woman for the whole evening at a party, with little or no regard for how you feel.
He may tease you playfully, or jokingly harass you or banter with you.	He will be deliberately hurtful, denigrating, or insulting.
He may show up late.	He'll be MIA. After he's missing in action for a week at a time, he'll pop back up on the radar and call you out of the blue and act like nothing is wrong. Usually the call will come late at night.

In a sense, there is no such thing as a "little bit" of disrespect. Because when a man sees that you'll accept a little, it entices him to even greater audacity. The fastest way to become despondent is to let someone push you around, because when you come out of the fog, you'll hate yourself for allowing it. So you have to identify what's happening before you can learn how to respond.

The first question becomes: Should you stand up for yourself verbally? Or nonverbally? To avoid playing into his hands, you have to be a bitch with your actions, not your words.

DESIRABILITY PRINCIPLE 57
Men *hear* what they *see*.

In the movie *Million Dollar Baby* Morgan Freeman said, "Sometimes the best way to throw a punch is to *take a step back*." The following sections will teach you how to gracefully do just that.

Female Button 1: He may attempt to make you jealous.

In England, there is a proverb: "A woman without jealousy is like a ball with no bounce." This may help explain why men use jealousy to test women. "How much bounce will she have? Will she be like a pinball machine with bells and whistles? Can I get away with murder if I buy her a dozen roses?" If so, that's great fun. For one person, that is. Men know competitiveness is a weakness of most women, which makes jealousy the Cadillac of all the buttons they can push.

One of the first things a man may do is try to convince you that all his ex-girlfriends still want him (even the one who ran off with another woman). His version? "I let her down easy, but she never got over me." If he spends the day at the zoo, the female gorilla wants him too. In other words, he wants to hoodwink you into believing every woman between the ages of eighteen and eighty wants him so you'll think he's a catch.

This is why he'll take you to a restaurant and be extra suave to the waitress. Or he'll glance at a woman at the movies. This is why he'll give an extra-long hug to a female friend right in front of you. And not the pat-on-the-back kind of hug, either. It's always the kind of hug that makes you want to spray-hose them down like you're breaking up a couple of dogs.

Carmen was dating Sam for several months. He wanted to see where he stood and decided to broach the subject by telling her about a new girl at work. "There's this girl in my department who is always hitting on me and leaving me notes." (The red flag is that he's announcing it. That's clue number one that it's nothing to be concerned about.) Carmen said, "I sympathize with you. And I know how annoying that can be. I have this body-builder guy who keeps bugging me too. He wants me to go to Europe with him, and I barely even know the guy."

DESIRABILITY PRINCIPLE 58

When a man tries to make you jealous, it rarely has anything to do with his desire for someone else.

. . . When you are upset he gets the reassurance that you care.

Think about it: If he truly had action on the side, would he be telling you? He may as well take out a billboard that says, "I have no action on the side *whatsoever*. And I get plenty of 'me' time in the shower." If a man does something *that* obvious—like leave a woman's business card in *plain view* where he knows you'll see it—he's most likely doing it to get attention and reassurance that you care. The card was put there so you would see it. If a man looks at another woman when you are six inches away from him, you can't be thinking, "Radar! Radar! Another woman is better than me. I am not good enough." He's doing it because he knows you'll pick up on it.

Therefore, apply the Hollywood axiom: *"No audience . . . no show."* If you don't provide a reaction you won't encourage and reinforce the bad behavior.

A classic example is Gary, who took Lindsay to a company Christmas party and then left her alone to go talk to a few attractive female co-workers. He stayed gone for forty minutes. What some women would have done is stand next to the punch bowl all night, pouting. But Lindsay adopted the "monkey see, monkey do" approach, and acquainted herself with the handsome single men in the room. When she spilled her drink, she was surrounded by men who were trying to pat her dry. Gary turned around, and described it as a "pack of wolves swooping in on my tender little sheep." His sidebar ended as he made a beeline back to his invited guest. Did he leave Lindsay alone at parties after that? Not a chance.

Another variation of the jealousy button is the guy who says, "You know, the one thing I miss about my ex is that she was a really good cook." Allow me to translate: He is hungry. He wants you to go to the kitchen and become the Iron Chef. He's hoping you'll make a big banquet fit for a king, all to compete with some fantasy ex that never even existed. He may say, "She kept a clean house." *Whatever he wants you to do more of, that's what she was allegedly good at.* This is why some men rave about their mother's cooking to their wives—to keep the hot meals coming.

A girlfriend of mine who is a single mother has a twelve-year-old son who visits his father regularly. Then he comes home and raves about his stepmother's cooking: "Candace makes the best fried fish." So you see, it starts early. (That's some unsuspecting little girl's future husband in training.)

This reminds me of a cute story about a girlfriend of mine. She convinced her husband that she was a gourmet cook without ever cooking him a meal. How? One day, she went to a yard sale and picked up a whole box of cooking items for ten dollars. She got a whole pot set, cooking timers, big syringes, and plenty of spatulas. She never cooked a day in her life. But it sure made a spiffy impression whenever he came over and all the pots were in plain view on the stove or kitchen sink. See? Just when you thought that a naked woman soaking in a bubble bath was their ultimate fantasy, you realize . . . pots 'n' bubbles is just as good.

It is often said that men marry their mothers. But they don't necessarily want a woman wearing an apron and bonnet baking fluffy muffins in the kitchen. It has more to do with "mother knowing best." In other words, they want a competent woman who can think for herself, handle her business, take charge, and tell him to knock off the foolishness—just like Mommy did when he was growing up.

When he's trying to make you jealous, he wants to see who is behind the wheel. When his little plan swirls out of control and he sees you take an unexpected detour, he pulls up the emergency brake and repositions himself. Then he begins to obey the driving rules, and from then on he drives like he has good sense.

Sophie was dating Tyler and they were in a committed relationship. Tyler told her about a female friend who, according to him, "wanted him." (Again, he's announcing it. It's obvious. That means she has nothing to worry about.) Sophie read the situation and responded calmly: "I don't want to interfere, and I wouldn't want you to make the wrong decision. If you want to see other people, that's fine. See if you like her and let me know when you've made your decision." Sophie hung up the phone, and the next day Tyler sent roses to her work. When she called to thank him, he invited her to go away for the weekend to a romantic hotel in Santa Barbara. The mystery woman's name never came up again.

If you don't react, guess what? Oops. The button has been permanently disconnected, and is no longer fun to push. If he continues to make innocent references to a particular ex-girlfriend repeatedly, all you have to do is put the shoe on the other foot. "Luke used to make me laugh all the time. And my folks just loved Luke." He will never see another *Star Wars* movie without cringing at the name Luke.

DESIRABILITY PRINCIPLE 59

**Once *you* start doing the same
thing *he* was doing, suddenly the bad behavior
will magically disappear.**

If you put the shoe on the other foot, does this mean you were "playing games"? Absolutely not. It was *his* game to begin with. He dragged you into it, kicking and screaming. He ran to first base, stole second, and rounded third. (You simply finished the game and brought him home.)

Female Button 2: He pulls back in some way.

Men are used to having the upper hand. When a man becomes a little standoffish, or he doesn't call, text, or see you as often, he's watching to see how persistent you'll become. Just like women play hard to get, men do the same. If he gets any inkling that you're willing to follow him around like a puppy, his next move may be to see if you'll "work for it" like a puppy jumping for a biscuit. (You have to let him know that your middle name ain't Sparky.)

That said, he *should* feel desired. He should feel valued, appreciated, and adored. Just not after he behaves badly; otherwise you'll create a monster.

A perfect example is Thomas, who was used to getting

a reaction from Faith after staying out late drinking with the boys. Faith asked him numerous times to call when he was out late. He didn't. This went on for a year. One Friday night he tiptoed in at 4:00 A.M., went to the refrigerator, and poured a couple of beers down the sink so it would look like he had come home earlier. After staging the crime scene with the empty bottles, he crashed on the couch. When he awoke Saturday morning, Faith was gone. A girlfriend who is a flight attendant called Faith and asked her if she'd like to hop a flight to Hawaii for the weekend. Thomas didn't know, and for the rest of the weekend he freaked out, panicked, and called her friends and family to locate Faith.

(Fast forward a day and a half.) Sunday night, Faith comes bouncing in with a tan, the smell of coconut oil, and a gorgeous lei around her neck. "Aloha!" Suddenly, there was a complete role reversal. "Why didn't you call? I was worried sick!" Then came a lecture about being more considerate. Faith listened while munching on Hawaiian Mauna Loa nuts. Then she responded, "I don't understand why you are giving me such a hard time. Didn't I bring you back some nuts? Besides, if you total up the hours you've stayed out late drinking in the past year, it wouldn't even be a fraction of the hours I was gone." Then she pranced upstairs to unpack. Thomas never forgot to call Faith again. He went out half as often, came in at a decent hour, and even bought her a fancy cell phone so they could always reach each other.

DESIRABILITY PRINCIPLE 60

When a man doesn't call, a bunch of scenarios will run through a woman's mind.
Similarly, his imagination will run wild also.

If you can't afford a trip to Hawaii and don't know any flight attendants, there is another, far less expensive alternative to deal with the "partner who rolls in just before dawn" dilemma. There is a new invention that is sold at Home Depot or any hardware store commonly referred to as a dead bolt. (When used once in very cold temperatures, it has a 99 percent effectiveness rate.)

When a man is coming in late or he doesn't call, he's in control. Some even play up the party-boy façade: "Oh, man, I am so hung over. We had so many mai tais last night." He probably had beer nuts, a stolen green olive from the bar, and one light beer. "If I stay out all night drinking, will she leave tread marks in the carpet from pacing back and forth?" So he'll act like he's a beer-drinking pig . . . and damn proud of it. Why? Because when he knows someone is waiting, worried and upset, he feels cared about. It's the same feeling you get when he sends roses, a limo, and tickets to the theater.

Even teenage boys do this with their mothers. Stevie, age thirteen, said, "If I know my mommy is going to yell at me, I may as well stay out at the arcade even later, and have another soda pop. If you call while you are out, you know you are going to get yelled at anyway. So why spoil all the fun? You may as well just get yelled at once when you get home, instead of getting yelled at twice."

On the other hand, if he comes home and you aren't even there for his grand entrance, it's no fun anymore. "Where is she? I didn't get my adrenaline kick. Wait, she doesn't care where I am or where I've been. Why *isn't* she upset?" I've even heard some men come right out and say, "I stay out late because it makes my girlfriend appreciate me more." (Her reaction reassures him she cares.)

As common as the "drinking late" scenario is the "working late" scenario. Brett was dating Andrea for a short while. He called and said he was thinking of canceling because of a grueling day at the office. It was left that he wanted to "play it by ear." When Brett called back at five o'clock, he had a second wind and wanted to get together, but Andrea had already made other plans. She then used the magic words: "I didn't want to make you feel any pressure. So, I made plans to go to a barbecue."

Remember this magic phrase: *I don't want you to feel any pressure.* It works like a charm with men who work really hard at their careers. Successful men explained that they are constantly fielding demands to do things out of obligation, pressure, and commitment to work. The last thing he needs when he's Donald Trumpin' is a lover who gives him more of the same. Be the exception to the rule.

If he has a legitimate reason for not calling, be understanding. If you do address it, the best thing you can do is be direct, use reasoning, and keep your response measured. This shows self-control. If a guy is late a couple of times, in a matter-of-fact tone say, "I noticed you're always late. So if we make a date, and you're not here by eight thirty, I'm going to run over to my favorite Pilates class that starts at eight thirty. At the very least, give me a heads-up so I don't miss you."

This is called a "truthful untruth." You are saying "give me a heads-up" instead of "call me" and telling him that you will make other plans if he keeps you hanging. The casual approach takes the "stink" off of it. Translation? Self-control.

DESIRABILITY PRINCIPLE 61

The more rational and calm you remain, the more emotional he will become.

And keep your radar antenna pulled up. If he says, "I lost track of time with the boys," or, "I completely forgot," that should signal your radar that he's doing it to get attention. If you give him some, he'll do it again, so act like you didn't even notice. The only time you *should* address it is if you had tentative plans and he held you up by not calling. Then lower the boom. How? With men, don't start with a long story that leads up to what you are going to say. That tells him you are unsure of yourself. Instead, just call it . . . fix it . . . and get over it.

1. **Call it.** "In the future, don't leave me hanging. My time is valuable to me, and there were a lot of other plans I could have made."	**Between the lines:** Note that you said *your* time is valuable. You aren't necessarily indicating your time *with him* is valuable.
2. **Fix it.** "Please give me the same courtesy that you would give to a client you work with."	**Between the lines:** You are equating the situation to a work example. (Lo and behold, a logical woman.)
3. **Get over it.** Now drop the subject like it never came up.	**Between the lines:** Translation: The negotiations are now over.

What a lot of men infer is that when you drop hints or beat around the bush, you don't feel comfortable enough with yourself or the communication in the relationship to speak your mind. When you state your case in two sentences, *and then drop it*, it demonstrates confidence. "Uh-oh. If I try that again, it will get me replaced." It makes him consider commitment much more strongly when he sees that you can't be trifled with.

DESIRABILITY PRINCIPLE 62

To a man, it is inappropriate to be emotional when talking about something important. If you speak calmly, he'll assume it's more important.

The first thing he will hear is your *tone* of voice, and only then will he give clout or credibility to the *content* of what you are saying. If your voice is supercharged with emotion, he will assume that even you don't know what is wrong. "She's emotional, so I'm just going to tune her out." Then he will hit the Mute button and tune you out. "She's under my thumb. I can do whatever I want and she'll still be there." Therefore, if you want him to hear you, you have to be very matter-of-fact.

The first thing a true fighter learns is that one must pick one's battles wisely. A champion fighter won't stand there swinging hard and slugging it out with a ninety-pound weakling. A good fighter knows that if he fights every battle, even if they are strong ones, he'll start losing because of battle fatigue.

So a way to avert a fight is to call him out, in one sentence or less.

In a matter-of-fact tone say,

> **"This is unnecessary, wouldn't you agree?"**

> **"Is this something you think is normal?"**

If he pretends to be confused, rephrase.

> **"Is this something you regularly do? I was just wondering."**

Then be silent. If he gives you a response that doesn't fly, say,

> **"I see."**

Then nod, take a sip of your cocktail, and change the subject.

Notice how you *aren't* being pulled in, but at the same time you are signaling that his behavior is unacceptable. Whenever you take the high road, others are quicker to feel low. When you don't give him a negative reaction, you aren't giving him anything to assuage his guilt. He can't put the "crazy mark" on you. He can't say, "She's a live wire. Look at her. She's attacking me for no good reason." That gives him an out, so he never has to examine his own behavior. *Or correct it.*

This reminds me of the motto from the movie *Primary Colors*, in which John Travolta plays a satiric version of former President Clinton. When he is asked why he won't do attack ads against his opponent and run a negative campaign, he quips, "I just don't want to give that son of a bitch the power to make *me* the son of a bitch."

Whenever you sense you are being pulled in, remember this saying: "Never wrestle with a pig. If you do, you'll both get filthy. But the difference is *the pig will love it*."

Female Button 3: He may say something off-color.

Part of testing is finding out where your unique buttons are. (Inquiring egos want to know.) So a man might put his boots up on your coffee table. He may use your pretty Ralph Lauren bathroom towel with the decorative pink bow on it to mop up around the toilet after he "sprays." As he grows more comfortable, he may emit a deadly plume of toxic or lethal fumes after eating chili. Or he may say something a little outrageous or off-color, like ask you to come over in a trench coat and high heels, to see how you'll react. It's all by design to see how you come at him.

One guy even admitted, "I sometimes say things to piss my girlfriend off because she looks so sexy when she's annoyed."

To show you how commonplace in the male "school of thought" that it is perfectly acceptable to deliberately provoke someone (even if you like him), I have excerpted a classic example from one of Donald Trump's books, *Trump: How to Get Rich*. Not only does he admit he tries to rile people, he advises his readers to do the same. Why? "To see what the reaction is." Here's what he says:

> *If you say something seemingly off the cuff, you may get a revealing response. I might make an outrageous comment in a meeting just to see whether the other people play along or take a stand and disagree. It's a good way of assessing the mettle of the folks across the table. Do they want to be liked? Are they comfortable with unpredictability? Are they capable of candor?*

Men do this all the time to get you to drop the "nice" veil, so they can see how you scrap. It's a little like what a carnivorous animal does when it's curious. It's called gumming. A bear will break into a car and then gently nibble on a small object to see what it is. Is it an animal? Is it still alive? Is it edible? What texture does it have? The bite is not a death blow. The bear just shakes it around a little and gives it a little nibble.

Where do men learn this? Let us now explore the origins of this learned behavior by getting in touch with his inner seventh-grader.

When a young boy is growing up, chances are he played a game on the playground called The Dozens. Basically, several boys gather around and begin to bag on one another. They exchange verbal potshots with precision:

Boy 1: "Your mom has an ass that's so big, it covers two whole zip codes."

Boy 2: "You don't look anything like your daddy."

Boy 3: "Your auntie has a flat face like a Pekingese dog."

If one of the little boys loses his cool or shows any sign of crying, whimpering, or cracking under pressure, *he gets kicked out of the game.* So they learn: Vulnerability equals hell. This game is also called Lemon Squeezer because a kid might want to cry but can't. So his facial expression will look like he just bit into a lemon because he's wincing and fighting back the tears. The winner is the little boy who kept his cool and had the most convincing comebacks. This is how men learn to trade verbal blows.

Adult men playfully abuse one another the very same way. They see it as emotional toughening and a male form of affection. If one guy shed a tear in 1986 because his team lost the playoffs, he'll never live it down at the weekly poker game.

"Hey, Bobby? I bought you a box of Kleenex tissues with your name on it. It's in the powder room . . . help yourself."

"Bobby, get me a beer from the kitchen while you are up. Don't forget my doily. Bobby just enrolled in cooking class. He likes being the bitch in the relationship."

"Bobby has a nice ass. Wouldn't he look good in a push-up bra?"

This is where his jokes come from when he roughhouses with you. It's his way of showing affection. It's his way of telling you he sees you as an equal. They think of it as a playful way of "romantically sparring with you." One guy explained, "You want a woman who'll joke around and be your partner in crime. No guy wants a yes-girl." He's looking to see if you'll be able to stand up for yourself *without falling apart*. If you can give it right back, he'll see you as a trusted partner. "This one is well rounded."

DESIRABILITY PRINCIPLE 63

Many men reduce women to a set of givens—that women are emotional, and that he'll be able to gain control if he finds her emotional buttons.

Most men rely on the fact that most women are emotional and that he'll be able to gain control, if he finds your emotional buttons . . . once he finds out where they are. When he can't, he'll often crumble and become the more vulnerable one in the relationship.

This is how men think. Most men assume women simply cannot be analytical, and that we are "technically challenged" in the sciences. I recall overhearing a few guys watching a news program that featured a female astronaut on a NASA space mission. One guy looked so spooked, the other guy began to console him. "Look, someone's gotta do the cookin' and washin' up there in space."

Men banter and say things in jest about women being in the police force too. And the military. Why? Women are too emotional, and emotional creatures can't be fully armed, especially with semi-automatic weapons. When the platoon goes out commando style, men are afraid that the girlie in the unit will get scared, cry, panic, and empty her automatic weapon in the wrong direction—and accidentally mow down half her platoon. If they could turn back the clocks, they would. All the women would have to turn in their rifles and get certified to carry vegetable peelers. During the dedication ceremony, you'd hear the trumpets play and the soldiers would be honored with Purple Heart pins. Then the "little ladies" would get little purple pots. "We hereby honor you for whipping up a great snack in the face of incoming mortars."

Yes, men tend to be a little predisposed. And when you surprise him with a reasoned approach, he'll think, "This one's got fire. She's a keeper." A lot of women don't realize that showing you have a brain and a mind of your own is often the way to win his trust and respect.

DESIRABILITY PRINCIPLE 64

He is testing to see if you believe in yourself. He wants to know who is at the controls. When you aren't easily shaken he sees, "This one can't be manipulated."

A girlfriend named Renee has a great comeback she always uses with her boyfriend. Sometimes, he'll call her in a crabby mood. To avert a spat, she'll end the conversation in a cute way. She'll say, "Have you eaten? You sound hungry. Go eat something, and don't call me back until you have a full belly." It's sort of like the one where men say, "Are you having PMS?" Only it's affectionate rather than insulting. And, the best part is that it can be used as a defense to his crabbiness during breakfast, lunch, dinner, and every hour in between.

A guy named Harold talked about what he finds irresistible in his feisty fiancée. "When I harass my fiancée verbally, she'll put me in my place." They were talking about marriage and he said, "Why buy the cow when you can get the milk for free?" Instead of getting defensive, his fiancée Robyn, laughed and came back with, "I know what you mean. Why buy the pig when all you want is a little sausage?"

Before he'll go on a roped bridge to cross from one mountaintop to another, he'll shake it to see how secure it is or whether it will fall apart. Men will watch to see how you do battle. "Is she a warrior? Or will she be din-din?" Before he becomes your knight in shining armor he wants to know, "Is she even worth defending?"

It's human nature. If a woman doesn't show she has a bit of stamina, men will see weakness. Men respect strength. Telling a woman a guy will protect her emotionally is like telling a little kid to walk up to a schoolyard bully on the first day of school and to tell him, "Here, take my lunch money. And you can have my cupcakes too." Or, in a dating situation, "Here, take my body. Take the home cooked food. Take dessert. I made you a cake. Please like me."

In the fight movie *Redbelt*, the teacher tells his female

student: "Conquer your fear, and you will conquer your opponent." The teacher later tells the class, "You think he has a handicap? No. The other guy has a handicap if he cannot control himself."

DESIRABILITY PRINCIPLE 65

Men may tell you about an alleged imperfection, to trigger your insecurity. If it doesn't trigger your insecurity, it will often trigger his.

Female Button 4: He may push the envelope.

A happily married woman of thirty-five years told me a story about her husband. When they were newlyweds, her husband would leave sopping wet towels everywhere. On the bed, on the floor, over the doors—you name it, there was a towel on it. When asking him to pick up his towels didn't work, she started throwing them out the second-floor window onto the "towel tree." Before every shower, he would go outside and pick a towel off his tree. Summer turned to winter and the towels were losing their "effervescent smell." And that's when he decided to comply with the U.N. household resolutions. (If it isn't in the hamper it does not get washed.)

What some men do is pretend they are incapable of doing something, so you'll always get stuck doing it. My girlfriend Julie is a good example of this. Her husband dressed their daughter in a green shirt, yellow shorts, and red socks. Julie wanted to say, "Are you color blind? She looks like Bozo!" But instead she said, "Oh, honey, thanks for getting the baby dressed while I showered. That was so thoughtful." Then she did a little damage control and changed the baby's socks while Big Daddy started the car.

Men do it all the time. They feign incompetence. They'll deliberately do a horrible job on the dishes, the laundry, and the ironing—to avoid being asked to do it again. If you criticize him about any domestic duties, parenting things, or stereotypically female chores, he'll say, "Fine. If I don't know what to do, then you do it." This is precisely the scenario you want to avoid because from then on, you'll get stuck doing it.

DESIRABILITY PRINCIPLE 66

To encourage the right behavior, state what you want, and then give him a way to fix it. Show him how he can be your hero.

Paulette did this with her husband, to a tee. She and her husband both work full-time. They have an understanding that whoever gets home first is the one who starts cooking dinner. Paulette said, "Whenever I pull up and I see he's not home, I keep driving and stay gone long enough for him to get the food ready. I pick up dessert, and then I rave about how good his cooking is. Now he does all the cooking."

If you want him to do the grocery shopping, appeal to his ego. Say, "I don't know what you like. And you are so much better at it than I am. You should go. Here's my list . . . ." When he gets back, tell him, "You are definitely the expert with this. Nobody does it better."

Strategic helplessness can be very *helpful*, indeed. Animals use similar diversionary tactics in the wild. When a mama duck has a brood of baby ducks and a predator is around, the duck creates a distraction by pretending to be wounded and flapping around everywhere. She steers the predator's attention away from the babies. And as soon as he's been lured far enough away from the little ones, she flies back to them.

Another rule of thumb when communicating with men: You should never say, "Honey, we need to talk." He will run for the hills like there's a hurricane warning.

Warning: *A flurry of feelings ahead.*

Outlook: *Not so good.*

Tonight's forecast: *Flannel muumuus, turbulence, and unexplained headaches in the bedroom.*

Pop psychologists tell you that if you don't want someone to feel attacked when you address a conflict, you should begin every sentence with "I *feel* . . ." rather than "You . . . ." With the male species, it pushes the right buttons a lot quicker if you leave feelings out of it and tell him what you *think*. When in Rome . . . talk like Romeo. Romeo would begin sentences with:

"I believe . . ."

"By my estimation . . ."

"My take is . . ."

"How I analyze the situation is . . ."

"Objectively speaking . . ."

You will get his immediate attention when you use non-emotional words (which he is completely unprepared for). Following are the seven words men love to use, interchangeably. I've included a quick-reference guide to the male definitions of these words.

A CRASH COURSE IN MALE-SPEAK

LOGICAL

Used when he endearingly describes you to all his buddies, over a few beers: "She is uncontrollable. Luckily for her, I am logical."

SENSIBLE

Sensible is another favorite. Men think women aren't sensible because they buy a lot of shoes and expensive handbags to impress other women. Men, on the other hand, are sensible. For example, he thinks it is "sensible" to buy a forty-thousand-dollar studded motorcycle, so that he can enjoy the benefits of internal bleeding (and irreversible hearing loss) while riding in style. It's even better when he's wearing two thousand dollars' worth of

Harley leather clothing so he can look stylish wearing that neck brace in the ambulance.

PRACTICAL

Men think that home items like throw pillows or decorative towels in the bathroom are ridiculous and "impractical." Curtains are impractical. Practical is what he insists he is being when he hangs up a Mexican serape from Tijuana in lieu of a curtain and then refers to it as "mood lighting." After all, nothing screams "do me" like a scratchy blanket covered in dog hair.

STRATEGIC

Men love the word *strategic*. "Since we both work, I think it would be a good move strategically if we employed a maid." The word *strategic* makes him feel like he is an important businessman, like he is El Presidente of the household. Not only this, it stirs up fond, soothing memories of when they were children playing with their miniature soldiers.

ANALYTICAL

An ability bestowed only upon the male species, to "analyze" how women are too emotional.

REASONABLE

His opinion.

UNREASONABLE

Your opinion.

Our male-speak class is now adjourned, but before you go, remember your homework assignment. Instead of "We need to talk about my feelings," say, "Let's analyze the situation *rationally* and *logically*." Now you are the one holding the remote and pushing all the buttons.

The first thing that will happen is that he will turn and look at you. Then he will look confused. He may look down to see if you are still genetically female. Then the lights will go on. Not only will it impress him, it will even make you look like you know what you are talking about. As for the look on his face? Priceless.

5

WANTED:

JOE PAYCHECK

Why Financial Independence Makes You Desirable as a Wife

I like compliments. But I prefer cash.

~ANONYMOUS

The Captain of My Gravy Train

There are certain things a man who is dating you will not come out and say. First and foremost, a man won't tell you that he's scared of having his clock cleaned in a divorce. Or that he's horrified of being stuck in a marriage with a woman who doesn't have sex with him, and makes him feel like an ATM machine. Or that he is valued only because of what he can provide. To a man, that is the worst kind of entrapment.

When I wondered what the subtitle of this book should be, I asked a couple of men for their input. One guy jokingly said, "It should be called *Why Men Marry Bitches: A Woman's Guide to Early Retirement*." Funny though it is, it speaks to the heart of what men fear most: a woman who is marrying because of her "business acumen." Not because of true love.

DESIRABILITY PRINCIPLE 67

When he's dating you, he'll constantly be on guard and watching to discern, "Does she like me for who I am? Or for what I can provide?"

When a man takes a bitchier, independent woman out to dinner, he's not thinking to himself, "Without me, she won't eat." If he takes her away for the weekend and he's discussing the $1.6 million real estate deal he closed, her response will be, "Good for you. Congratulations." But she won't seem terribly impressed or hungry to get a piece of it. If he picks her up in a $350,000 Aston Martin, she'll get into the car and say, "Thank you for picking me up. It was thoughtful of you to drive so far out of your way." *This shows that she appreciates him, not the car.* This is the woman who will make a man get out of his "me, myself, and I" mode and get him thinking in "we" mode. Why? Because she is *unimpressed* by the shallow things most women are impressed by. This sets her apart.

It's your independence that wins his heart. He marries the woman who lets him know she'd sooner be picked up in a used Dodge with dents in the side and hubcaps missing, than to be treated with disrespect. If he has a bad attitude or isn't a gentleman, he has to know you will hail a cab or take the bus home. It's when he feels you can't be "bought" that he thinks about marriage.

When it comes to marriage, men tend to shy away from women who know all the expensive hot spots. Or a woman who name-drops, and is all too familiar with accoutrements of success. When she says, "Nice Rolex!" what he sees is a potential shakedown on his horizon.

Ever seen those want-ads where a woman places an ad looking for a "generous man" to "take care of her"? What the guy's read is, "I'm selling myself like a used Buick with a bad transmission." It doesn't matter what else that ad says.

She can talk about walks on the beach until the cows come home. All he'll see is a financial agenda. Here's what he'll interpret when reading between the lines:

WANTED: JOE PAYCHECK

Do you have a house I can take? Are you plenty happy being a working fool and handing over all your money? If so, I've got a prize package for you featuring three interest-earning babies so I can expand my retirement portfolio. If you call now, I promise to tell all my girlfriends you're hung like a three-hundred-pound llama, even if you are hung like a light switch. Plus, I'll even convert to make the in-laws happy. I am an equal opportunist. So hurry, I'll be standing by with all my bonbons.

A quality guy won't say, "Gee, where do I sign up for that?" Remember, bitch stands for **B**abe **I**n **T**otal **C**ontrol of **H**erself. It doesn't stand for **B**ecause **I** **T**ook **C**harlie's **H**ouse.

DESIRABILITY PRINCIPLE 68

When a man sees you are focused on your own dreams or on elevating yourself, he feels safer marrying you because he doesn't worry about what you'll be trying to take *away from him*.

Men, more than ever, are warming up to the idea that a woman who can contribute financially can be an important asset, especially during tough economic times. He marries a woman who has depth. Men worry about making ends meet and what you would do if he fell short of cash.

Men are secretly afraid of being inadequate and of showing their weak side. They are afraid that after they woo you, and they turn out to be less than the Prince Charming fantasy you fell in love with, you'll up and split. Rest assured, men have dreams of finding that special girl to spend the rest of their lives with. But in his dreams, his partner is someone *he can count on*. This is why a bitch appeals to men. She's more real, she doesn't buy into his BS. She's less likely to bolt when he drops his veil.

Men don't talk about this need for "security" because it's not considered manly. It's taboo. But they want the feeling of security also. Here's what runs through his mind when he thinks about marrying you:

> "Would she grab the next available cash cow
> if I was struggling financially?"

> "Would she be able to hold down the fort
> if there was an emergency?"*

> "Would she leave me for a guy with
> a new Mercedes and a bigger house?"

> *This one is a biggie.

Men tend to approach love as though it's a business-deal negotiation. One of the most common things I heard in my interviews with men was the question, "What is she bringing to the table other than sex?" Here's where the bitch quotient comes in again. Men usually label a weaker woman as a liability and a stronger woman as an asset. It's just like business school when there is an acquisition and they calculate the "value added." His knee-jerk observation goes something like this:

LIABILITY:	ASSET:
A woman who is desperately looking for a guy to rescue her from her life. Her only goal is, "I need a boyfriend." "It will be like adopting a child I'll need to take care of. She needs someone to pay the bills."	A strong woman with goals, who won't give herself away. Then he feels, "She really loves me for who I am. She's not with me because she needs a meal ticket or a daddy."

As Will Smith said, "Competence is the thing that is most attractive." Men regularly said the same thing: They want a woman who can TCB (**T**ake **C**are of **B**usiness). It turns them on mentally and sexually also. It gives him something men aren't supposed to need: a feeling of protection and safety.

This is not just for his benefit, but for a woman's benefit. I like something that I heard Lady Gaga say: "Some women choose to follow men, and some women choose to follow their dreams. If you're wondering which way to go, remember that your career will never wake up and tell you that it doesn't love you anymore."

The upshot is that it actually turns men on as well. When he meets a woman who can buy her own cup of coffee, she exudes a do-it-yourself attitude that immediately earns his respect. Men are drawn to women who see themselves as winners. Some men don't mind the *option* of taking care of someone after falling in love. There is a difference between an *option* and an *obligation*. He doesn't want an *obligation* forced on him.

Peter recalled his early impressions of his wife, Kim. "She was a native-born Chinese woman who came here from another country and didn't even speak the language. She started her own business and became successful. And that's pretty amazing, considering the fact that she didn't speak a word of English when she arrived." I asked him if Kim's traditional upbringing made her submissive in their relationship. "Oh, hell no. She doesn't put up with any crap from me. Not for a second." Notice what he respects: Kim's strength of character. The only time she'll take a handout is when it's coming from her *other* hand.

Another true story. A successful banker told me a story of when he knew he wanted to marry his fiancée. She is an RN at reputable hospital who specializes in treating premature infants. One day she took him on a "ride-along" where he got to see what she did for the day. He describes that day as a defining moment in their relationship. He said, "I got to see what she does. I saw her do little baby chest pumps (then showed me with two fingers how she performed CPR and his eyes literally lit up). I could tell doctors spoke to her with respect. That was when I thought, 'Man, I am so lucky to be with this girl.'"

You often hear men admit to being mentally stimulated when they see a woman "in her element." Whether it is the clothing business, the medical industry, the legal profession, hearing her talk to a client on the phone, or just seeing her in professional clothing, they secretly respect a woman who is doing something positive and constructive.

Now compare this to a woman who isn't building anything other than a wardrobe, got everything from her parents or men in her life, and comes into a relationship with a sense of entitlement. She is pretty, but then she starts talking about her "goddess" energy or her "diva-like" qualities, and wants the "finer things" in life to be handed to her on a silver platter. Or she'll use the word *queen* or *princess*: "I am a princess. Any man of mine has to *worship* the ground I walk on. And he has to worship my dog too." Then she orders the most expensive wine on the menu because "she's worth it" and poses on a barstool as if she's Queen Elizabeth having her portrait painted. All of which comes back to bite her in his exit speech. "Dating me is not going to be fair to you. As a goddess, you deserve so much more. I can't treat you the way you deserve to be treated and I would hate to see you suffer. I think we need to take a break from dating."

A friend of mine named Bobby said, "Sometimes you feel like you want to ask a girl, 'Hey, uh, could you bring your credit-card statements to our next date? I want to know what kind of *lifestyle you've become accustomed to* before things get too serious. Are you a cash burner? Do you spend three times what you make?'"

DESIRABILITY PRINCIPLE 69

Men don't judge how much money you have. They notice *how you budget* what you do have.

As early as the first date, he'll be imagining what his life would be like if he stepped inside your world. So he'll start fact gathering and recording everything in his memory bank, like a video camera with two legs. Here's what he'll record:

The Marriage "Risk Assessment"
Things men notice:

- ✓ If you carry a three-thousand-dollar designer purse (with fifty cents inside).
- ✓ If you have a new car that is all scraped up and looks like a rolling storage unit.
- ✓ If your place is clean and inviting or unkempt (he'll assume that's what he'll come home to every day).
- ✓ If you have a huge stack of old bills on the countertop.
- ✓ If you have knobs missing off the TV or stereo (he'll assume you break things).
- ✓ Whether your animals are well taken care of.
- ✓ Whether you have a rotation of roommates who don't stick around very long (this means you are hard to live with).
- ✓ If the electricity or phone gets turned off (he infers he'll be adopting a young girl who will constantly need to be taken care of).

✓ If you are paying the cell bill with a maxed-out credit card and the collection agents are knocking at your door (you'll screw up his credit).

✓ If you have a closet crammed with shoes and clothes and tons of makeup scattered everywhere in the bathroom (your appearance is all you have to offer).

✓ If you don't return videos on time, or if you bounce checks.

✓ If you keep a well-stocked bar but have no food in the refrigerator (you might be a party girl, and not really suitable to live with).

✓ If you borrow money, or use the word "help" and have to rely on friends or family to make ends meet.

✓ If you've been married before and made out like a bandit in the divorce (he'll be worried that he's about to get dusted off as well).

Why do these signals make or break your marriage potential? These are clues that tell him whether you can build a life together. He's looking for signs of neglect because he wants to see how you'll treat the things he will work hard to provide. He won't comment on it, bring your attention to it, or break up over it. But he'll store everything in his memory and weigh the information heavily when deciding to move forward with marriage.

Most women think they have to worry about the guy's finances because he's the so-called provider. But today more than ever, men are looking at your finances also. Yes, even the wealthy ones. It's often the deciding factor for whether he will marry a woman.

The *Leave It to Beaver* standards have changed because of how much the cost of living has gone up. Back in the 1950s or 1960s, a Cadillac cost five thousand dollars and a home cost fifty thousand. Times are different. Now that same Cadillac costs fifty thousand and a decent house in a metropolitan area can easily cost a half a million to a million, or more.

A really successful man named Kenny explained: "Women are taught they just have to be pretty, and a guy will take care of them. I've known women who made very little money, and lived in one-room apartments. But every time a bill needed to be sent out, it was sent out on time. She managed with what she had. She didn't dig herself into a hole. I've also known women who had a lot of money, but spent it on nonsense like two-hundred-dollar face creams with fetus protein in it, or a five-hundred-dollar dress. Two weeks later she cried because the electricity was turned off. Or she ran out of gas with her BMW, and had to walk to the gas station in a Chanel outfit. Then she acted like the whole world was picking on her. That's the type of woman who will put you in an early grave."

DESIRABILITY PRINCIPLE 70

Men admire women who want to elevate themselves and pull themselves up by their own bootstraps, and fear women who are social climbers at a man's expense.

It can often be the reason he'll call off a wedding. Lee and Tracy are a perfect example of this. She was a hairstylist living with a roommate, and Lee was a very successful entrepreneur. She had dreams of owning her own salon, and Lee admired that. After nine months they got engaged, and he gave her a gorgeous canary diamond engagement ring. He also told her he'd pay for the wedding. She chose the Ritz-Carlton, a twenty-thousand-dollar Vera Wang gown, and Tiffany's for the wedding registry. All the guests would be treated to a night at the Ritz with a complimentary facial or back massage (on his dime). The only thing that he told her he objected to was the Tiffany registry because he worried his working-class relatives wouldn't be able to afford the high-ticket gift items on her list.

Lee recalled, "I couldn't get my mind wrapped around why anyone would need to register for a nine-hundred-dollar Tiffany crystal punch bowl. I started to feel uneasy and it made me question the situation I was about to step into. When she quit her job, I realized I was making a huge mistake and broke off the engagement. I didn't feel like the wedding was about a true blue 'love thing' and that we'd be taking on the world together through thick and thin. It became about putting on a show for all her friends. It wasn't a life together that she wanted to build. It was a very expensive fairy tale she wanted me to pay for."

Since men don't usually share the Cinderella wedding fantasy, try to be mindful of how your anticipation looks to a guy. Men notice when a woman who has nothing of her own suddenly develops very expensive taste.

If you aren't self-sufficient (or *working* toward being self-sufficient), everything you say about commitment and marriage will be looked at with suspicion.

SHE ASKS:	HE HEARS:
"What are we doing for the holidays?"	"I can't wait to meet my new in-laws!"
"Do you own a home?"	"I want to give a thirty-day notice and move in."
"Can I borrow your car?"	"Can I drive my new car?"
"Do you ever think about getting married?"	"I can't wait to quit my job."
"What are your intentions?"	"Where's my ring?"
"I refuse to waste my time."	"I bought the dress. Time's up. Let's set a date!"

This is what frustrates men, because they rarely hear a woman say, "I can't wait to start a business." Or, "I can't wait to take that real-estate class." With most women, their goals are, "I want to be married within one year." So she goes to the gym, buys makeup, looks fabulous, and doesn't understand why the relationship isn't moving forward.

Remember the classic scene from *My Cousin Vinny*? Marisa Tomei's character asks Vinny when they are going to get married: "My clock is ticking like this . . . [*stomp, stomp, stomp*]." It was great in the movie, but in real life this is the last thing he wants: a woman who is stomping her feet and who is pissed off because she can't believe she is being cheated out of the marriage she's *owed*. Men are so frustrated by this, they even have slang phrases they use with one another describe it.

"On a mission." Defined as any woman who wants to fall in love with a beautiful wedding, and isn't nearly as concerned about whether she's in love with the groom.

"Filling a position." The feeling he gets when he realizes her interest in marriage has nothing to do with him.

This is why you instantly become the one who is "different from all the rest" when you don't act like marriage is the holy grail.

The whole biological-clock thing is not just about babies. Women are socialized to believe that they have a shelf life, sexually. And, women buy into it. They don't see themselves as a prize after a certain age. When I spoke with men about the pressure on women to be married by a certain age, I was surprised to hear most men say this was a myth. If a woman takes care of herself, she can be sexy in her thirties, forties, fifties, and beyond. There is no "shelf life" for marriage. According to men, what makes a woman less desirable is the insecurity surrounding her sexuality, not the lack of it. Or, when a woman thinks *the only thing she has to offer is sex.* If a woman is twenty years old, attractive, and has her whole life in front of her, but she thinks her only bargaining chip is "I have a nice rack" or "look how cute my butt looks in these jeans," she will quickly become boring. If that's all she has to offer, if she isn't competent, spicy, and independent, that's what will make her less desirable.

Whenever I met a happily married man, I always made a point of asking what it was that made his wife different. Michael shared the following story. "When I met my wife, she held a prestigious position with an ad agency. Then she lost her job. So she waited on tables until she found a replacement job. She never took the 'oh, poor pitiful me' attitude. She was realistic. The bills needed to be paid, and she grabbed the bull by the horns. I respected her because she rolled with life's punches. And I knew then I could build a life with her." He was won over by how she handled adversity. It was her character that won him over. Even when times were tough, she wanted to stand on her own two feet.

This affects how a husband treats a wife after they are married too. Eva is happily married, and until recently her husband was the breadwinner. When she wanted to buy something from the Home Shopping Network, she would ask her husband. Sometimes he'd say, "Let's wait a week," which sounds a lot like something you'd say to a child: "Wait until you save up your allowance and then I'll buy that for you." So one day, without asking "prior permission," she took the initiative and got a part-time job. Now, instead of "Can I buy this?" she walks in and says, "Honey, look what I bought." And a funny thing happened. Eva noticed her husband's passion went through the roof.

Men feel more emotionally connected to a woman who can be a little authoritative sometimes. The woman who can get up and leave at any time is the one who can put him in check. When a man meets a competent woman who doesn't need him, he instantly treats her *differently* than the woman who seems unsure of what she wants out of life. That's the woman he marries.

DESIRABILITY PRINCIPLE 71

He doesn't want to marry a helpless little girl whom he will have to take care of.

The helpless or frail woman who can't make decisions will quickly turn him off in the bedroom also.

Although there is an exception to every rule. Once in a blue moon, you'll come across a guy who wants a helpless wife or a "little girl" who will stay in the kitchen and bake cookies. This is why some men get a mail-order bride. Of course, his drastic decision to marry a foreigner usually comes on the heels of a horrifying experience (like dating an American woman who used too many big words). So he swears off American women and runs off to a distant land to meet the bride of his dreams. (Just as soon as he's done getting a few hair plugs put in.) And it is pure bliss, just like they promised in the . . .

Mail-Order Bride Catalog

Your Blushing Bride Comes with the Following Tender Moments . . .

She doesn't speak a word of English. Therefore, she will never voice an opinion or disagree. She will simply give you dirty looks and use expletives in her native tongue when you don't allow her to go to the prom.

If you have TiVo, you can eliminate the horrible documentaries about the "Women's Movement" and show her the finer things in life: Shake 'n Bake.

The vows will be nondenominational. "Do you promise to obey . . . and obey . . . and obey, until immigration status do you part?"

At the reception, we'll provide a rum cake for all the adults. We'll also provide Puddin' Pops for the bride and her classmates.

We'll even give you a sentimental gift, gratis, from our wedding registry. You can choose from either a harness, a swing, or a swatting paddle for the honeymoon at Disney World.

It's true. You never hear about a messy divorce with a mail-order bride. She stays until the green card comes. After that, she goes to the market to buy a quart of milk and is never seen or heard from again. *Poof!* She disappears into thin air like a mafia turncoat entering a witness protection program.

Obviously, men who marry mail-order brides are taking advantage of these women's economic situation. Sex trafficking is illegal because the trafficker takes a woman's liberty and keeps her against her will. But bringing a new bride (who is a virtual stranger) from another country is legal— even though it is an extortionate relationship because she would be forced to go home without a green card, and she is forced into sexual submission.

That's not a marriage. That's exploitation masquerading as a marriage.

For most men, they want someone who wants them. Men don't want a helpless little Stepford Wife. If he has a lot going for him, he wants a partner who desires him. One who will have his back. When he sees that a woman can make good decisions in her own life, he will instantly feel closer to her. "Cool. We are like-minded." That's the woman he'll take with him to pick out a starter home, new carpet, and new furniture. She becomes an asset. A man likes a woman who knows her own mind, who can think, especially if he trusts her. Because then a lot of pressure is lifted off him when he doesn't have to always make all the decisions.

DESIRABILITY PRINCIPLE 72

**For a man, the words *respect* and *trust*
are interchangeable. If he doesn't respect you,
he will not trust you.**

. . . and without trust, he will always keep you at arm's
length.

Appreciation: The Inroad to His Heart

More than food, more than sex—whether you make a
man feel appreciated when you are seriously dating will
often make or break whether he ties the knot. And that's
another thing you never hear about in a woman's magazine. Appreciation is the way to a man's heart. He'll go to
the ends of the earth just to have a woman make him feel
adored. Mary Kay Ash said, "There are two things people
want more than sex and money . . . recognition and praise."

Sometimes a guy will do something for you, like bring
a gift, buy flowers, run errands with you, put gas in your
car. When he does small things and you don't say, "That
was so thoughtful. Thank you," he will start to give less.
Eventually, whatever he gives will become mechanical—
offered with little or no real feeling on his part. His feelings
will wither away until he disconnects altogether.

This is why men stay late at work and avoid going
home to their wives. It's why they stop making an effort.

Nothing will demotivate him faster than feeling that he's unappreciated.

DESIRABILITY PRINCIPLE 73

**When he gives you something,
always acknowledge the kindness behind
the gesture, not the material item itself.**

Just like women can't get too many compliments, a man can't get too much appreciation for his contribution. Danny told a story about a woman he had wined and dined for several months. One weekend, she invited him over for a steak dinner to reciprocate. When he got to her house and opened the fridge, he noticed there were two items inside: mustard and stale bread. Debra said, "I meant to get to the grocery store. Could we go to the market?" He accompanied her into the market and started pushing a cart for her. She grabbed a second cart and announced, "We're going to need both." She then proceeded to pack both carts to full-tilt capacity. The carts were so heavy that she could barely push hers through the checkout stand. The bill? Close to two hundred dollars.

Danny said, "I paid for it all, and she never thanked me or even acknowledged it. To top it off, she didn't even cook me a decent dinner. She opened a Value Pak and made me a four-ounce piece of chicken. [Danny is a big guy who is known for being quite generous.] The sixteen-ounce steaks I picked out mysteriously vanished. I don't know who ate the steaks, but it wasn't me." When I asked him if he ever took her out again, he said, "I'd sooner date a mugger who wore a ski mask and robbed me at gunpoint."

When I interviewed men, this was one of the biggest reasons that they had reservations about marriage. If you want to *talk a man out of* being generous, all you have to do is create the impression that what he just gave was consumed, vaporized, and absorbed with very little appreciation. It's the quickest way to take the fun out of his courting you. As one man put it, "Your days will be numbered."

DESIRABILITY PRINCIPLE 74

A man's favorite word is *appreciate*. He wants more than anything to feel revered and valued. When she's appreciative, it motivates him to give her the world.

When you act like you appreciate his accomplishments, what he did for you, what he gave to you, and so on—this is the most important validation he can get. This explains why men will forget a birthday, an anniversary, and Mother's Day . . . but they'll never miss a "coach of the year" award ceremony to get that crummy little trophy cup.

He won't hand over his heart on a platter, buy a ring, pay for a wedding, and give you a house if you wolf down a dinner like it meant nothing to you. Therefore, if you want him to give you the stars, the sun, and the moon (and the pear-shaped diamond), be sure to acknowledge what he did and make a fuss over it, and then say the magic words.

"I appreciate your fixing [whatever he fixed].
It is so helpful."

"It was really fun the other night at [wherever he
took you]. Thanks again."

"I absolutely love [a gift he gave you, even if you
hated it]. Thank you again."

Then add:

"Thank you, that was so generous of you. I love this.
Thank you."

Or, "That was thoughtful of you to think of me.
Thank you."

Or, "That was really considerate of you. I really
appreciate your thoughtfulness. Thank you."

Look at the words above, and commit them to memory. These should become staples in your vocabulary, because there are no sweeter words to a man's ears.

This is where many women go wrong after the wedding as well. They take too much, and base it on what *they think* the guy can afford, and disregard his input.

I recently heard two very successful doctors talking. His wife had just given birth. He refused to have another child with her. His friend asked him, "How's she doing?" The doctor responded bitterly: "She's doing great, because she has a *full-time* nanny so she can do nothing all day. She goes to Pilates, goes shopping, has her hair done, and she has her toes painted." At that point the other doctor tried to make light of it. "Look at the bright side. At least she isn't demanding a chauffeur driven stretch limousine, with the baby and nanny in their own separate limo."

If a man is the breadwinner, she does not work and they only have one child, he will probably question why a full-time nanny is a **primary** childcare provider to his child. Had she continued to work part time, or had she said "I don't need a full-time nanny, honey, a part-time nanny is enough," she might have appeared more reasonable. Instead, he was working 80 hours a week at two hospitals, while she went to Pilates to "relax."

DESIRABILITY PRINCIPLE 75

Most men aren't looking for an *equal* contribution, just a *fair* contribution. By contributing in a reasonable way, you maintain his respect and trust.

When I talk to successful men who started out being very generous, you could cut their sadness with a knife. It's not about money. It's about the loss of his dream. A woman's dream is to grow up and marry her prince. His dream is to "build his empire." That's why he goes to college, starts a business, works hard, invests well, and buys property. He's building his empire. His wife is a big part of that empire.

If the woman he is with is not helping him financially . . . or has more children than he can afford to support . . . if she doesn't pitch in with childcare . . . if she never cooks or cleans . . . or if she piles unnecessary bills on his shoulders . . . he may start to feel she is severely damaging how he envisions his "empire" should fold. If there is a pile-on effect, he may emotionally check out of that relationship. He will not only feel duped and betrayed, but also saddened. It's much deeper than money. In order for a man to work decade after decade 40, 60, or 80 hours a week, he has to believe in a cause. If he thinks she's the reason his *empire* will never come to fruition, it's a game changer. Each day he goes to work, he will do it with a feeling of resentment because now he's a slave to a cause that *he no longer believes in.*

If you don't believe me, ask any hardworking man.

Another variation is the guy who has his own business, and his wife won't help. He has to pay a full-time receptionist, bookkeeper, or assistant—to bring home half the profits, while she goes shopping.

DESIRABILITY PRINCIPLE 76

If a man feels taken advantage of, he will check out and there will be no emotional connection.

After all, partnership is about sharing your life together. A man who feels he may have met his soul mate will not be that obsessed with what he spends, as long as he thinks you aren't taking advantage of him. If he likes you, the only thing he'll care about is getting your affections. As one man explained, "It's a good feeling to a guy to be the generous one, and to be able to take a woman out when you are in love with her."

Coupons, refunds, splitting plates, or a severe reluctance to pick up the tab—all of these should not go unnoticed, because he's showing you he doesn't really take the relationship seriously. As one man explained, "A guy cannot be madly in love with you and be really cheap at the same time." And if he is just a cheap bastard? You wouldn't want to be with him anyway. Imagine what those wedding vows would sound like. (A trailer-trash moment to behold.) "I promise to love and honor . . . in sickness and in health . . . until death do us part . . . unless I have to drop twenty dollars and then I'm outta here!"

Playing House

Vanessa met Jean Marc and they had a whirlwind courtship. Three months later, he professed his love, bought her a ring, and they decided to live together. She sold her condo, quit her job, and moved into his place an hour away. Soon after, she started noticing a change. Whereas before, he was respectful, he slowly became condescending toward her. Nine months later, she moved back out. Trivia question: What's wrong with this picture? Everything.

First is the timing issue. You never want to move in with a man after a few months or relocate to his stomping grounds. That's just way too soon. Also, when you move into his place, his "bachelor pad" is rarely going to be conducive for two. Because of this, it is highly unlikely that you will ever really feel like it's your place too. It will feel like a slumber party gone horribly wrong. If you try to change his place around to make it more suitable, he'll start feeling like he's giving up too much of his space. And you'll have to part with a lot of the stuff that makes you feel comfortable in your own home. All in all, not a good situation.

DESIRABILITY PRINCIPLE 77

When you move into someone else's place, you don't just give up your personal space and belongings. More important, nearly always you also *lose your feeling of independence.*

When you bring two cats home together as kittens, they get along well. But if you bring a cat into another cat's territory, the cat whose territory it is will dominate the other little cat from then on. This is why women feel off balance when they move to a man's turf. It's a territorial thing.

Therefore, either let him move into your place (if there's enough room) or, better yet, go look for a place that is new to both of you. That is the best-case scenario because you'll be able to negotiate for everything you need. A closet of your own . . . a bathroom of your own . . . and anything else that floats your boat. And I highly recommend a king-size bed. Not for you. For him. It's the considerate, loving thing to do. It will prevent you from accidentally strangling him in your sleep because he hogs the bed and leaves you just enough room to dangle off the lower left corner of the queen mattress. Trust me: king size.

Let's assume he does have an enormous house, with a California king bed, and you move in. And let's say he's a multimillionaire with stupid money, and you end up quitting your job. At some point you still run the risk of having an argument, only to have him turn and say, "Where do you think you would be if you didn't have me? Look around. I provide you with *all of this*." This is precisely what you want to avoid. So the best thing to do is move into a new place *you both choose* together. Then, maintain your independence. Keep your job. Keep your friends. And definitely keep your own bank account and your own credit cards. It will give you the leverage to be treated how you want to be treated: with equality and justice for all.

Also, one quick final note:

DESIRABILITY PRINCIPLE 78

If marriage is extremely important to you and you are ready to set a wedding date, don't move in unless you have a ring and a date.

If he's already "playing house," he won't have a reason to accelerate the process or take that next step.

Shotgun Weddings

This chapter would not be complete without one final discussion about pregnancy as it relates to marriage. It happens all the time and no one likes to talk about it. Yes, we are going to "go there."

Malena was dating a successful oncologist for six months. During that time, he was very good to her, but he made it very clear he didn't want children right away. Six months went by, and he hadn't proposed. Malena became increasingly impatient and "accidentally" got pregnant. Later, she admitted that she went off the Pill because they made her queasy (neglecting to mention that until it was too late). He tried everything to persuade her to terminate the pregnancy. In the end, she had her daughter and he turned out to be a great father. Just one glitch: He wanted nothing more to do with her.

Having a baby is one of life's biggest responsibilities, and you should never knowingly have a baby with someone if he *makes it a point to tell you* he doesn't want to be a father. You simply can't have a relationship based on mutual consideration and at the same time nullify a guy's right to make such an important choice. The reason it backfires speaks to the "attitude of entitlement" that men repeatedly said was a deal killer—whether it's a nice dinner, living together, or marriage and kids. After Malena dropped her bombshell, to him she became the most unattractive woman in the world.

The father of the baby explained why it ruined her chances for marriage. "It's wonderful to have sex, right? But what if a man was to force you against your will? It would not be so wonderful anymore. That's how a guy feels about an unwanted pregnancy that he suspects is deliberate. If she shanghais the guy into it, he may love the child. But he will feel nothing but resentment toward the woman every time he looks at her. At that point she becomes frightening. What it tells him is that there is something very dangerous about her and that she is capable of anything. That's the woman who will sleep with your best friend and think nothing of it. Once a woman crosses a certain line, the odds of him marrying her, or even continuing to see her, are slim to none."

Men ultimately respect a bitch. Why? She's not a bitch because she's having a bad day. She's a bitch because she's a principled person who lives by her values. Standing up for yourself is one part of the equation. Being a stand-up person is the other part.

I've also heard several men tell stories about being engaged. And sometimes, during a heated blowup, some men ask for the ring back. In one instance, the guy's fiancée said no and claimed she had lost the ring (coincidentally that day). The next day, a mutual friend confided in him that she had pawned it. After that, the relationship was on again . . . off again.

She still wanted to get married, and for six months they had "break-up sex." But he refused to make a commitment because he couldn't get past feeling duped about the ring. Here's how most men think: If you appear honorable and say, "Here, I want you to have this ring back," he will say, "No, you keep it." His pride won't let him take it. But if you have a sense of entitlement or make him feel taken advantage of, he will want the ring.

If a man has any kind of substance and isn't as deep as a puddle, he'll have a couple of morals. What earns his respect is *decency*. Whenever I spoke with men about what they were looking for in a wife, I never once heard, "She has to be a good cook," or, "She has to wear Victoria's Secret lingerie every night." Instead what I heard time and time again was, "I want someone I can trust and count on."

DESIRABILITY PRINCIPLE 79

The biggest turn-on for a man is knowing that he is in love with a woman he can really count on, who will *really* be there for him.

6

BREAKING INTO
THE
Boys Club

Stolen Secrets—All the Highly Classified Things Men Will Share Only in the Company of Other Men

A good marriage depends on the husband's ability to take a step back, and see where his wife is wrong.

~ARCHIE BUNKER

Highly Classified Secrets from My Covert Operatives

Brace yourself. This chapter will give you a rare glimpse inside the minds of some of the men I interviewed. As you'll witness, my information-gathering techniques would stump even Dirty Harry. Much of my scientific training was acquired in a very controlled setting. It began with a diet soda, a large bowl of popcorn, and watching back-to-back episodes of *Wildlife Journal* on Animal Planet.

In this chapter, you will hear the chattering of the male species from deep within the trenches of the dating jungle. To record the primates speaking, I did what any zoologist would do: I approached the creatures in a very nonthreatening way. I also learned not to approach during feeding time, for fear that they would growl and retreat back into their habitats for the winter.

I am also happy to report that my interrogations did not require any torture methods like the use of bright lights, sleep deprivation, electric prods, or playing reruns of *Little House on the Prairie*. Nor were they forced to watch *Ghost* with looped scenes of Demi Moore whimpering over her clay pot. I used no coercive methods whatsoever. At no time did I resort to the most horrifying threat of all: removal of one battery from the remote control.

We, here, at the headquarters of Bitches-R-Us, do not believe in animal testing. Therefore, no men were harmed *physically*. (I cannot comment on their current mental state.)

I now present to you my first subject. His name is Timmy. He is nine years old.

Sherry: How old are you, Timmy?
Timmy: I am nine years old.
Sherry: Can I interview you? I am writing a book.
Timmy: I am going to write a book too.
Sherry: What's the title?
Timmy: *Why Girls Are Dumb.*
Sherry: I hear you have a girlfriend. Is that true?
Timmy: Yes, her name is Sandy. And I know she has a
          crush on me.
Sherry: How do you know?
Timmy: Because she's really nice to all the boys . . . but
          she's really mean to me.

Timmy was the youngest of my interviewees. As men get older, they get more guarded about what they are willing to divulge to their partners. They feel that if they show their hand all the time, they'll lose control over their relationships. After all, certain sensitive subjects don't exactly make for good dinner conversation.

Most men were very open, but others were less comfortable revealing their secrets. I found that the guys who were "commitment material" were far more willing to talk about the types of tricks many of their friends use on women. I came to realize it's a little bit like breaking the law.

(When you are doing something illegal, you don't want to go telling everyone about it.) That confirmed what I already knew: Men have a secret code with respect to commitment, marriage, and the inner workings of relationships.

I've excerpted some of the most truthful confessions in this chapter, verbatim. Here is what my "covert operatives" revealed. The men were from all walks of life, all nationalities, and all ages. Some were married, others were single. And with the exception of nine-year-old Timmy, I've withheld their names and identities (to protect the not-so-innocent).

Question 1: Do men mislead women about wanting commitment and marriage to get certain sexual "benefits"?

"Absolutely. A THOUSAND PERCENT."

"All guys know that their girlfriend will be more sexually responsive and more emotionally understanding if she is made to believe their relationship has 'long-term potential.' All you have to do is use the right buzzwords, like *we* or *our* or *future* or *probably someday*. Men routinely use this to their advantage. 'I bet I could get her to do X, if I told her I was thinking of marrying her. *Someday*.'"

"If a man is seeing a woman, she'll usually let you know what she wants to hear. She projects to him what she needs to be told, and he says it. She makes the bed and he lies in it. It isn't until a year later she will start to get frustrated because she's not seeing any progress. He won't move in with you, he won't give you a key to his place, he won't even leave you alone in his place, and she doesn't have a ring. That's when she starts seeing that the relationship has reached its ceiling."

"Women think they are being sneaky, but if she's trying to drag me to a wedding every other Saturday, it's hardly subtle. If she starts putting pictures of the two of you everywhere, that is obvious as well. Let him be the one to put the picture up, otherwise he'll see it as the old fire-hydrant marking."

"Guys are tricky. If they have a big house in a nice area, they'll often use it as a hook. He may ask you to help pick out the paint for the 'baby room.' For when you have a kid together *someday*. And if periwinkle blue doesn't work out, it can always be one hell of a game room. Or he'll ask you to help him pick out furniture. If you tell a woman that you just bought a house and you need help decorating it, she'll practically handcuff herself to you. And your bedpost."

"Men have relationships with women out of state. And women always think it's going to lead to something more. It won't. The guy gets off the plane, has sex all weekend, and then goes home. You can justify the come-and-go because you live in a different city. There's a built in excuse. Guys refer to this as a *long distance friend . . . with benefits*."

"Guys are sneaky. We have one friend who told his girl-friend, 'The only way I would get married is if a woman woke me up with a BJ every single morning.' The poor girl wore herself out every morning for three years, and he never proposed."

"What a man will do is tell the woman she's intelligent, funny, sophisticated, and that he's interested in her mind, and her soul (as he pulls her thong down). Essentially the goal is to make her feel like you don't see her as a sexual object. Then she thinks, 'Finally, a man who sees me as more than an object!' and she jumps in the sack with you. Men do it all the time. The goal is for her not to know what you are really after."

"Men act like the perfect lover boy. You'll say something like, 'I've never cheated on anyone. I'm not a kid anymore. My days of running with the boys are over, and I'm looking for something *real*. I'm more settled now and I have my eye out for Mrs. Right. I feel different with you. I feel like I could confide in you things that I couldn't confide in anyone else.' When a guy comes on that strong, be careful. Usually the opposite is true. And if that's well delivered, he has most likely said it many times before."

"Some guys will call a lot, or seem very interested in boring conversation. I've actually fallen asleep during phone calls and woke up and said, 'Really? Then what happened?' And when a guy isn't really listening, that's a sign he's not interested in you. He's just biding his time until he gets into your pants."

There are two things to glean. First, if the wrong guy has too good a read on what you want (marriage, commitment, or material things), he'll use it to manipulate you. Pay close attention to the guy who said, "It's like giving a guy a manual on how to manipulate you. All he has to do is tell you what you want to hear, and it will take you a couple of years to figure it out."

A married man named Gene explained, "When a woman says, 'If you want to date me, you have to propose by the end of the year,' it goes over about as well as someone saying, 'I just wanted to go out tonight because I didn't feel like being at home.' In other words, the only thing he edged out was a rerun of *Seinfeld*. Instantly, you back off when you *aren't the reason* they are there." Set your own timelines and limits, and leave if it's time to get out. Until then, don't let him know about your timelines or deal breakers. Then keep your eyes open and watch how he manages his 50 percent of the relationship. Then you'll get the real deal much quicker.

Question 2: How would you describe the traits of a confident woman (aka bitch) versus an insecure woman?

"The worst thing a woman can do is see a guy every night of the week. That's how she becomes his good-time girl on his 'reserve list.' What will happen is, the guy will start coming over at nine o'clock and then he'll leave by ten thirty. If he gets access or what he wants from her anytime he wants it, he won't have to lift a finger to keep it going."

"Men are competitive. When he buys a car that is a limited-edition model, he feels like he has something special. Guys in the street who race cars usually race for pink slips because they want to win, conquer, and take the other vehicle. That carries over to women. A woman who is easy won't scratch his competitive itch. When she stops expressing her opinion and starts agreeing with everything he says, that's usually when a man starts to feel bored."

"A woman should never go looking for him or chase him down at three different places where he said he *might* be having a drink. If he says, 'Either I'll be at the Cheesecake Factory or some bar on Twenty-sixth,' don't try to track him down. If you want to be his 'steady,' let him come track you down."

"My fiancée was the first woman to put me in my place. She constantly reminds me, 'Hey, nobody's forcing you to stay.' If I try to BS my way out of a situation, she'd say, 'Let me save you the time and energy. Don't give me that shit, because I ain't buying it.' I know if she caught me cheating she'd smack me over the head with a frying pan. And I respect her more than any woman I've ever known."

"If he can sum you up in one sentence, he'll be bored."

"Confidence is when you don't try to interpret or overly process everything that you are observing out loud. It prevents the relationship from progressing on a normal course. For example, every time I gave this woman flowers, she would remind me that her ex stopped bringing her flowers. What she really wanted to ask was whether I'd keep doing it in the future. That made me feel like she didn't really enjoy the flowers, or appreciate the present moment with me."

"A woman shouldn't say, 'You don't call me enough,' or, 'You never tell me you love me.' As a woman, your best asset is to be unpredictable. He should never be able to figure you out. When he can always predict what you are going to do next, you've lost him as a long-term partner. *He'll look for someone else, whom he can't understand or control.*"

"If she feels strongly about something, she'll have a backbone. This woman is the woman he respects. Not a 'melba toast' cracker that crumbles with very little pressure."

"You have to seem like you aren't giving yourself fully. 'Here I am. Take me.' Men want to be kept guessing. Think about it. When a guy picks out a movie, he wants to be on the edge of his seat from the very beginning. If someone doesn't lose a limb or get shot and buildings aren't blown up all within the first twenty minutes, he'll think he got cheated out of twenty bucks."

"A woman shouldn't even crack a joke about marriage. I was on a second date with a girl and we are both from Ireland. Back home we have a saying, 'If you kiss me you are going to have to marry me.' If you have the desire to get married, never let a man know that up front. If you do, it's the same as handing him a manual and telling him exactly how to dangle a carrot and play on your weaknesses."

Question 3: What are the signs that a woman is wasting her time?

"When you get the nagging feeling you are always left hanging. If he's closing doors, saying things like 'gotta go' or 'talk to you later,' that means, 'I'll call you when it's your turn.' And don't listen to the 'I missed you so much' nonsense he tells you when he's coming around for sex. He won't disappear for a week at a time with a woman he's committed to."

"If he sees you one hour a week, it's casual. If you aren't going to the movies, meeting his friends, eating dinner together, and he says, 'I'm really not much of a phone guy' when he doesn't call—it is clear. With a woman he cares about, there will be consistent contact. A man will rarely break dates with a woman he's in love with."

"What a lot of guys do is say he's too busy working. Work never gets in the way of who he really wants to be with in his personal life. If a man really wants to see a woman, free time will magically appear."

"If a man is truly busy, he'll be specific about when he'll call you back. 'I'm tied up right now, but I will call you back X.' Then he specifies a date and time. But if he says, 'I'll get back to you,' and doesn't say when, that is a sign of disrespect. If he was out of town, same rule applies. If he can't reach you he'll pinpoint a day he'll be inaccessible—not a whole week."

"When you start hearing that the cell battery went dead, or the cell reception wasn't good, or he left his cell phone in his car or at the office, he's telling you that you are as close as he is comfortable getting. He doesn't plan to get closer to you or move things along."

"If it's been over two years and he won't give you a key to his apartment, you haven't met anyone from his family, and he won't discuss living together or marriage, it's not progressing because he doesn't want it to."

"A lot of guys keep women on a 'reserve list.' If he knows you'll always be there, he'll think, 'I know that one wants me, so let me put her on the reserve list and see who else is out there.' This is why you can never be too available, or let the guy get *too comfortable*. He has to worry that you won't be there."

"If a man says, 'Let's just keep things the way they are,' he's pretty much telling you that he doesn't see marriage on the horizon."

"When the relationship is based on comfort and familiarity from the very beginning, there will be no effort. You can tell from the little things a man does or how he acts when he's around her. Does he walk her to her car? Will he drive out of his way? Or does he pull up to the curb and beep? And don't drive to his place in the late evening. It's a fool's errand."

"What a lot of guys will do is the 'jewelry store drive-by' with ring promised but not purchased. Or they'll look at a bridal magazine and say, 'You'd make a much prettier bride than her.' Then he has to get a promotion or a raise before he can afford to go through with it."

DESIRABILITY PRINCIPLE 80

A guy who really thinks you could be "the one" will say very little about marriage. He'll slowly open up over the course of several months, because he won't want to scare you off.

If he says things like, "Marriage is so antiquated. It's just a piece of paper. It's not really necessary. I have friends who have kids and have never gotten married. Who needs marriage?" keep him as a friend to go see a movie with, and don't close off your options.

Question 4: What secrets do men keep with regard to sex?

"Don't believe everything a guy tells you, especially in bed. One guy I know told a girl while they were having sex,

'I've always wondered what married sex feels like. Oh, baby. This is what it feels like to make love to my future wife. You are my dream. You are my shadow. Look at what you do to me.' It was the most sickening thing I've ever heard. No guy tells a woman he loves her and wants to marry her for the first time during sex. If a woman hears, 'I think I love you,' for the first time during a bump-and-grind session, she should end the sex right there. That's a total con artist she's in bed with."

"The reason men watch shows like *Sex and the City* and *Desperate Housewives* is to learn about women. They worry, 'Is that what my girlfriend is really like?' It scares men that women are so fixated on these shows. We want to believe she's too innocent to be fascinated by anything that decadent."

"Never discuss your past, or your lack of a sexual past. A man doesn't want to think about another man on top of you working up a sweat. Whenever someone is trying to convince you they are a 'good girl,' there's a 90 percent chance that the opposite is true, so anything you say will make you look guilty. He'll think you knocked boots with the whole football team in high school and they retired *your* jersey when you graduated."

"If a woman gives a fantastic blow job the first time you are together, and she does it without hardly batting an eyelash, he'll be thinking, 'Where the hell did she learn how to do this?' If you seem like a pro, you might be a 'ho.'"

"If you sleep with him right away, he probably won't be around very long. With a one-night stand, deep down you *aren't doing something you are proud of.* You know that's not how it's supposed to be."

"Men don't tell women that half the things they see in porn are a bit silly and over the top. If the woman is screaming, 'Give it to me, Daddy' in bed, immediately I'll be concerned that she has a troubled past."

"A lot of women think pillow talk consists of confessions wrapped up in self-pity. After sex, you don't want to hear about what a woman doesn't like about herself or have to be the one to make her feel confident. I had one girl say, 'I wish my legs were longer from my knees to my ankles. And I hate my hips because they are so wide.' It tells the guy she has low self-worth and that she's easily taken advantage of."

"Sometimes a guy will call late and try to have sex with a woman. It may piss him off because she didn't say, 'Sure, come on over.' But the next day he feels more interested in her because she's not a fool. She keeps him honest and doesn't roll over and acquiesce to every whim."

"When a guy is in bed with a woman, if he's really turned on and he doesn't want to climax, he'll start thinking of things like sports, being in a locker room with a bunch of sweaty guys after a rugby game, yard work, and that leaky sink downstairs . . . anything to take his mind off the moment. He does not want to earn the title of 'five-minute man.'"

"I don't understand the appeal of the little-girl outfits. If a woman wears her hair in little braids at age thirty-five, and she has a little dog named Binky dressed in a pink sweater and matching jacket and a rhinestone leash, that's not going to get me in the mood. If a guy is into nasty little-girl stuff, he shouldn't be left alone with children unless he's closely supervised."

A lot of the men admitted that although the "instant gratification" part of them wants to have sex on the first date, if they really want to have a lasting relationship, they prefer to wait. He really wants that diamond of a woman, someone whom he can really be proud of. If he ends up in the sack with you on the first date, he won't see you as "the one." Moreover, when he tells you all the things *he thinks* you want to hear, and you seem unimpressed or nonchalant, he'll usually start to pursue you on a more honest level.

Question 5: Why do men test women? And is it done purposefully?

"Yes, it's conscious. The reason men test women is we believe that if you are going to be spending your life with someone, you really have to see who she is from all sides. You want to know if she's crazier than a road lizard, or whether she'll be compatible with you."

"Most men see women as too emotional. This is why he'll give you a rundown of all his ex-girlfriends. While some escape with just being called a drama queen, others are labeled psychos (otherwise known as schizos). Every guy talks about that one psycho ex, with that one episode in which she lost it, and the men in white coats had to come and throw a net over her, and shoot her with a tranquilizer dart. You know, just like they do with a dangerous animal that escaped from the zoo."

"What a guy will do is watch a woman when another woman walks in the room. If she's the least bit jealous it will show all over her face. Then all he has to do is say that that woman has on a pretty dress, or she has nice hair, or she has a nice walk. And he knows that is all it takes to set off his girlfriend. She'll get so pissed, steam will be coming off of her. The truth is, he doesn't really give a damn about the other woman, he just wants to rile up his girlfriend. It may sound immature, but we want to know you still care."

"Let's say you've made a statement that you don't like it when someone is late. That gets stored in his memory bank. If he wants to test you, he'll show up an hour late with a good story. If you scream, shout, or curse, he won't think of you as marriage material. A calm reaction is, 'I was a little worried about you, but I'm glad you are here. Give me a call next time.' That tells you she is classy and graceful and, most important, she can be reasoned with. And that's the woman you'll consider marrying."

"Don't ask, 'Do I look fat in these jeans?' A guy might answer, 'Not too fat. Just stop eating all that ice cream.' What he's doing is keeping you insecure so that you'll work harder to please him. A lot of men think that giving luke-warm compliments to a woman makes it easier for them to manipulate her. If you need to be complimented constantly, men will assume you aren't secure with yourself."

"Part of a guy feeling comfortable with a woman has to do with how she treats him after he screws up. It's a little like dealing with your mother. Every man knows when he's doing something wrong. If I do something out of line, and my wife doesn't go to the gutter to address it, it wins my respect. That's a big turn-on to a guy."

"When a guy is in love, he won't go out drinking or fishing as much. But he still wants to do it every once in a while. If he wants to go to a strip bar, he understands that it's disrespectful. But if he wants to go to a football game, be supportive. Ask if you can get any hot dogs for the tail-gating party. This way he'll be thinking that marriage to you will be a lot of fun, and that he won't be missing out on the other things he enjoys."

"A woman cannot go off and have emotional outbursts all the time. He'll slowly lose respect for her, especially if she does it in front of his children. The most unattractive thing a woman can do is stomp her feet like a child. You don't ever want him to think of you like that."

"It's extremely important for a man to maintain his love and lust for a woman. If there's always drama, his sexual attraction will slowly turn off like a dimmer switch. Every time she is reasonable, strong, and rational—it makes a man want to give her the world."

"You have to be willing (or at least pretend to be willing) to listen to what he has to say. When a man feels he's really being listened to, or understood, that gives him hope that you can have a positive outcome. He has to think you don't rush to judgment, and that you'll listen. Even when he's telling you a bunch of BS, you can still listen. That gives you more credibility when you say, 'No chance in hell I'm ever going to buy that crap. If this ever happens again, I suggest you come up with a better excuse than that because that BS is not going to fly.'"

Now that you've heard it directly from the horse's mouth, remember not to get your panties in a ruffle. He's not doing it to get a perverse thrill, but rather to get attention. It's like a toddler in a high chair who throws his rattle down on the floor. Why? So Mommy will come pick it up. Then Mommy comes and picks it up and gives the rattle back to the toddler. And what does the toddler do? He throws it down again. Why? To get attention.

DESIRABILITY PRINCIPLE 81

The more control you have over yourself, the more of a hold you will have on his heart.

A person with self-control is a person who can get up and leave at any time. Men instinctively know this, which is why self-control raises the benchmark of how he treats you. Adopt the attitude, "I refuse to walk around like an exposed raw nerve. I've made up my mind that I'm going to be upbeat, positive, and I won't believe what other people tell me about myself." This is true empowerment and confidence. And it not only makes you a man magnet, it will make you a people magnet as well.

Question 6: What are men secretly afraid of?

"Men are afraid of being stuck with the wrong woman, particularly someone who makes him miserable. He's afraid she'll nag him like his mom did, and start looking like his grandmother did. He's not afraid of a wrinkle or two. He's afraid she'll transform into someone he doesn't recognize, who he couldn't imagine going to bed with."

"Men are afraid of having to compete with your BOB (**B**attery **O**perated **B**oyfriend). He wants to believe his magic pole is doing the job, and if you use BOB in front of him and it gets the job done quicker and better, he's going to lose his desire because he knows he can't compete with that."

"Men are afraid of showing weakness. If I've had a really crappy day, I may not want to talk about 'feelings' with my partner. I might even avoid seeing her altogether because I don't want to take it out on her. As a man, you want to be strong for a woman you care about."

"He's afraid of a woman driving his car. Men feel that most women don't appreciate equipment and fine crafts-manship. A man's car is his pride and joy. It never fails. A woman will open a door onto a curb and crash it right into a newsstand. But if he really loves a woman, he'll let her drive the car. Once or twice. It's a symbolic gesture. That means he trusts her and values her more than the car."

"Men are afraid of losing status or of falling apart emo-tionally, and not being able to pull himself together. That's why men meet at the campfire to cowboy up. Once you have a couple of beers with the guys, your problems tend to go away. That's why men don't want to see themselves lying on some shrink's couch, with someone handing him a tissue."

"A guy's biggest fear is that his wife will cheat on him. Most men are very afraid of that happening, especially after there are children involved. Men have thoughts that run through their minds. He knows if it ever happened, he would be faced with having to weigh the emotional welfare of his children versus his own emotional welfare. It's the kind of thing that ruins lives."

"I'm deadly afraid of having stupid kids. That's why I couldn't marry a woman who had a blank stare. No guy wants a glassed-over look, or a lifeless woman with no spark. You know the type—the ones where you begin to wonder if there was too much inbreeding with the cousins."

"Men want to have a good-looking wife, but they are afraid of being held to the same standard. Men wouldn't be able to handle it if he was crazy about a woman and was put under the same scrutiny. If his wife said, 'Hey, you are starting to have a potbelly, and I'm not feeling so attracted to you.' That would make him feel the heat, and he'd head straight to the gym."

"Men are afraid to be made into suckers, fools, or to be taken advantage of. No guy wants to be suckered into becoming a meal ticket. If you are a meal ticket, you feel cheap. Then you have resentment that begins to grow, and you start to feel that all women can't be trusted."

"Men fear divorce, because it's a woman's world in the divorce court. And if you have kids, your goose is cooked."

The pressure to be "manly" will influence how he approaches a relationship. Remember, men don't have different feelings from women, just a different style. It doesn't matter how unemotional they seem, men are vulnerable as well. They, too, can get squashed like a grape. A man has a deep need to be validated, and he often won't tell you when he feels vulnerable. If he's bothered he'll say, "Aw, hey, that's no problem," even though he could be crying on the inside.

DESIRABILITY PRINCIPLE 82

If a man really cares, he feels vulnerable. That's when he needs a protective shield the most and that's when he'll often behave more coolly.

Question 7: What is the best way for a woman to reignite a man's interest if it might be starting to cool off?

"She shouldn't."

"If a guy isn't keeping up the routine of what he's doing, she should stop all the calls. Make him think you lost interest, and become scarce. She should become unavailable and stop sleeping with him. He needs to think, 'Wait a minute? She usually calls by now.'"

"It's the old saying, 'You don't miss the water till the well runs dry.' Cut off the water supply with no explanation and no reason. The best thing a woman can do is cut off contact with no explanation and let him come through with a grand gesture."

"If a guy staggers in at 3:00 A.M., don't be home when he gets home. Call up a girlfriend and stay over at her place. That will be an instant wake-up call."

"One guy I know would stop off to have a drink every day after work. Then he'd wait for his girlfriend to start calling him and beg, 'Come home. When are you coming home?' One time she didn't call. He started calling the house and the phone just rang. Then he got up and ran home looking for her. Suddenly, going home became interesting. But as long as she was waiting on him, he was bored."

"One girl I dated would say to me, 'I'll call you right back, in five minutes. I'm right in the middle of something.' Then I wouldn't hear from her. That's when I realized I was taking her for granted and redoubled my efforts."

"To rekindle his interest, split for the weekend with the girls. Tell him you are going on a trip and don't call while you're gone."

"She can call him out. She can say, 'Listen, if I'm taking up your time here, and you are feeling like you'd rather be somewhere else, that's cool. There's someone out there for everyone.' If she recognized it and called him on it, it lets him know that she's in tune to what's going on and she isn't too accepting of disrespect. That keeps him on his toes."

"Pick up your own hobby. Don't wait on him. Get busy with something else so he is unsure when he can see you."

"You never want to be like a dog that waits at the door. An animal will wait for you because it makes its day. If you become like that, you'll become disinteresting. But if you always explore new things, and he can see you are growing independently, he will respect you. There's nothing more attractive than a woman who is passionate about her own life and discovers new things. He'll work to be a part of that, and he'll work to keep himself just as interesting."

DESIRABILITY PRINCIPLE 83

Whenever boredom sets in, simply break the routine. As soon as the routine changes, it will pique his interest.

. . . and the relationship will become interesting again.

Question 8: How can a woman tell if a man's really in love and thinking about forever?

"He's thinking for two, not one. He'll create things to do, and he'll be thinking for two—rather than thinking for one. He'll start making important life choices with you in mind. Where he lives, what house he buys, the trips he takes. The bachelor outings will become a once-in-a-while thing to see his friends for an occasional pool game. You'll become his favorite best friend to spend time with. If he has one week of vacation, he's planning it with you, not his long-lost buddy from college."

"His interest will be consistent. If he's thinking long-term, there won't be severed contact. He won't give his time sporadically and he won't contact you every now and then. On the other hand, when everything else in the world comes before you and you start hearing, 'My second cousin's brother's father-in-law's sister needs me to watch the kids, so I can't see you all weekend,' it's not about love. When he truly cares, you won't get the on-again, off-again intermittent contact. You'll have continuous access and you'll know all aspects of his life."

"He'll be on his toes a little with her. When a guy cares about you, he's much more alert and wants to please you. He has a certain sweat and a nervousness about him. You can call him any time of the day and ask him for something. If you walk up on a puddle of water, you get the feeling that he would throw his jacket over it. You aren't just taking up physical space like a piece of furniture. You occupy his mind and his thoughts also, and he feels a little tingle when he's with you."

"He won't give excuses. There will be no degrees and levels to love. No 'I love you but I'm not *in* love with you.' When a man is in love, he may have a bad day every now and then, but he doesn't waffle about wanting to be with you. If someone is separating love into different categories, making distinctions between love with a cherry on top and love with only whipped cream, then that's not love."

"If he really enjoys talking to you at the end of the day, that's a huge sign. When a man is in love with you, he'll call almost every day throughout the week, not just on weekends. When you drive somewhere or go to dinner, you never run out of things to talk about."

"He won't ask you out by always saying, 'Feel free to stop by.' He'll want to see you on an appointment basis because it's special. He'll be thinking, 'Let me build up to this. Let me drag this out.' That's when you know you are a prize—not just a piece."

"He'll be in your corner, even when you are wrong. His friends won't be able to put you down, and he'll be protective of your feelings. If a female co-worker calls him at midnight, he will ask her not to call that late. You will always feel like you are number one in his life."

"He will give you open access to his life. You won't get less attention after six months than he gave in the first month. At a certain point, he'll even let you answer his phone. Almost anything he does, you'll be invited to do with him."

"He'll go out of his way. With a woman he's crazy about, he'll put in all the overtime in the world. He'll be doing things for you, he'll be considerate, he'll want to please you, he'll try to cheer you up if you are down, and he will enjoy every moment because you are the person he values most."

"He'll ask you to marry him."

Above all, *he will respect you as a woman*. When a man is in love with you, he'll never refer to you as a "chick" or a "girl" or "his old lady" or his "ball and chain." He'll refer to you as his woman, or his girlfriend, or his wife, or his fiancée. He'll refer to you *with respect*, because he sees you as the girl of his dreams.

7

Q & A FROM
Readers

Frequently Asked Questions

*Never allow someone to be your priority while
allowing yourself to be their option.*

~NINA POTTS-JEFFERIES

Crazy in Love

I often hear men say that all women are crazy or emotionally unstable. Some men even break it down by category. In their view, women range from mildly irrational . . . to completely psychotic. Men have been known to get together for a few rounds of golf, or a few beers, and exchange notes on the mental health of their newest acquaintance. "I met a new girl, and she seems like she's in charge of her hormones." Perhaps you've noticed that there's always an ex-girlfriend he speaks of. You know, that one ex who snapped and became possessed by demons, causing the demise of their relationship. Of course, he never had anything to do with it. He was a perfect angel . . . and lo and behold . . . one day he woke up next to the Exorcist.

Maybe this is why women blame themselves for everything. I've lost count of how many times I have heard from women, "I keep screwing up my relationships. I feel like there's something wrong with me." They get the mental analysis from the boyfriend (the self-appointed therapist) and before long, she's second-guessing herself. "He tells me I am acting crazy. And that I'm not normal. I feel like I'm a little crazy." Then she picks up a two-by-four and beats herself with it. Over and over.

It's important to remember that marriage is forever. Dating is not for someone to put their stamp of approval on you. It's a time for you to assess who you are marrying, and whether he is worthy.

DESIRABILITY PRINCIPLE 84

When a woman can laugh at herself and doesn't take things personally, she seems more stable.

This chapter is designed to help the woman who is nice to everyone . . . except herself. She believes everything negative that happens to her is *her own fault*. To help you control your emotions (or, as men say, "remain in charge of your hormones") it might help to read what other women are experiencing. The following dating scenarios might sound familiar . . .

Dear Sherry,
In the beginning, Greg pursued me and said lot of romantic things. He told me he wanted to be remarried in Fiji. At a dinner, he massaged my left hand and asked, "When you wear jewelry, do you prefer gold, white gold,

or platinum?" (Fast forward a month.) Suddenly, he couldn't recall the things he had said. (Common form of "male amnesia"; symptoms include forgetting everything he said prior to having sex.) This confused me. I didn't reveal my goals and I followed your advice. How was he able to manipulate me?

Sincerely,

Robin

This is a good question, because it's not just about what you say, it's how you act. Let's assume you say nothing about marriage, kids, your future together, and living happily ever after. Instead, he says something warm and fuzzy. If a guy sees your eyes widen and your face light up every time he talks about weddings, houses, kids, or his future with you—it doesn't matter who brings it up. It can't be written all over your face. Men will smell your desire for a commitment faster. He'll smell it like a shark smells a wounded seal pup with a broken flipper, bleeding in the ocean. Sharks can literally smell one drop of blood five miles away.

Let's go back to that "romantic and wonderful" beginning because this is where the miscommunication started. It's not that men don't eventually fall in love, because they do. But that happens *later*. Even when you see a man who is married, with a minivan, and a Baby-Bjorn hammock and a newborn swinging off his back . . . that was not what he set out to achieve. At first, the game-plan was to get the woman's clothes off. He's a red-blooded creature with plenty of testosterone. And because of *his hormones* . . . he only has three emotions:

- Crabby
- Hungry
- Horny

. . . and not in that order.

Put another way, a guy will be very nice and charming, if he thinks you will sleep with him. It's verbal foreplay. You wear perfume . . . he opens the car door . . . you tell him you've only had three lovers in your whole entire life . . . and he tells you he is looking for a relationship and you have all the qualities the other women didn't have. It's a sales pitch.

Here is an analogy. Think of him the way you would a trained animal performing tricks in front of a live audience. Like a seal, or a sea otter at Sea World. When a seal balances a beach ball on the end of its nose, he's not trying to demonstrate how well-coordinated he is. And the seal isn't doing the tricks to impress the audience. He's doing it for one reason only: to get a salmon.

Same goes for men: If he buys dinner and sends flowers, he's balancing a ball on his nose. Some men do it better than others . . . and some seals can even clap three times while the ball is on their nose. But it's all being done for the same reason: to get a reward. If he wants to get the "treat," he has to do the "trick."

Women say, "I refuse to sleep with a guy who is not interested in a serious relationship." That's ammo for him to use against you. If he saw one episode of *Sex and the City*, or read one woman's magazine or relationship book, he knows that using key phrases about "love and commitment" is a one-way ticket to the bedroom. Men watch that stuff to learn what women want to hear, so they can promise those things.

One man named Bradley explained: "Men say very little and women 'grab onto it.' A guy could just be making a simple statement and next thing you know she thinks her dreams are coming true."

DESIRABILITY PRINCIPLE 85

Men don't believe they mislead women. Men believe that women mislead themselves.

If he disappoints you, he doesn't feel guilty. He'll rationalize, "She's not upset over me. She's upset because her plan ain't working." Now, that doesn't mean he doesn't like you, adore you, and think you are the sexiest thing in his eyes. What it means is that to keep the sex coming, men will mislead you about their level of intended involvement regarding commitment and marriage. Therefore, believe none of what he tells you in the beginning. Your job in the beginning is to keep him curious and let him get attached. After he's attached? That's when the negotiations can commence.

A Hint of Indifference Hooks Him

There's a way to get a relationship, but sleeping with the guy right away and trying to put a poodle leash around his neck is not the way to go about it. Instead, you have to knock him off his stride. How? By keeping your level of interest apparent, but not blatantly obvious. Why? Because it's what he is not used to seeing.

In the beginning, all it takes is a **hint of indifference**. This is always a trigger. If a man can't tell where you're coming from (completely) and doesn't have assurances of what you want, he respects you more and treats you better. Period. Why? Because he doesn't have the "pull" or control he's used to having.

You have to be able to sit next to a man while hugging and kissing . . . and at the same you have to *keep yourself emotionally ten feet away*. Even if you are sitting in his lap, your heart has to stay locked in the trunk of your car—next to the spare tire. You can be warm and affectionate. But stop telling yourself "He is the one!" And stop rationalizing, "He is different. He makes me feel something I haven't felt in years." Instead, you have to think: "I'm willing to learn more. I'm enjoying myself, but if it doesn't work out, there are other ducks on the pond."

Most women start off on "tilt" because they show they care *too* much *too* soon. Soon after, she's freefalling (by herself) after which he makes the following observation: "She is not in control of her emotions." Or as one man named Connor explained, "When I meet a woman and take her out a few times, I'm wondering, 'Who is in control? Her . . . or her emotions?'" If it's your emotions, you will be at his mercy. It's a guy thing. They learn very early that showing too much emotion is the same as showing weakness. When I spoke to men, this phrase came up a lot. "You can't show weakness . . . this is a sign of weakness . . . that is a sign of weakness." The good news is that most women he's met showed him plenty of weakness, so if you are mildly weak by comparison, you still come out ahead.

Let's compare:

Formula for Failure:

No Emotional Control = Desperation to Keep Him =

A Free Ride for Him

On the flip side:

DESIRABILITY PRINCIPLE 86

If you have the emotional discipline and self-control, you will have more control over how you are treated and how much you are respected.

I remember a conversation with my mother when I was in college. I was the age where women think they know everything and their mothers know nothing. I was visiting my parents for the holidays. Sometimes, I would say something ridiculous and I would hear my mother's mischievous giggle while she shook her head to herself, thinking of a way to tell me whatever she thought I needed to learn. After ten minutes I would have to ask, "What is so funny?" Finally, she would tell me. This was one of those examples.

I was complaining about a guy who I didn't even like much, and only went out with a couple of times. I complained to my mother that I couldn't get his "respect." My mother started laughing that mischievous giggle and shaking her head. I finally asked her what was so funny. She said, "If you are waiting for someone else to respect you, you'll be waiting a *very loooooong time*." Then she told me to "think about it" while she watched her favorite TV show.

A half hour later, when the show was over, I asked her, "Mom, why will I be waiting *a loooooong time*?" My mother said, "You can never let someone else dictate how you feel about yourself. You want respect? You have to *respect yourself*." At that point, I began telling her that I do respect myself. She cut me off. "No you don't. Because if you did, you wouldn't surround yourself with anyone who doesn't respect you."

The lesson I gleaned at a young age is this: whose responsibility is it that a woman is treated with respect? Do we empower a man to make that choice? Or do we make it our own responsibility? That turning point in my life inspired the next principle.

DESIRABILITY PRINCIPLE 87

If someone doesn't appear to respect you, don't waste a moment of your time on them.

There is nothing for you to gain. Many women think it's their fault someone doesn't respect them. I've come to realize that 90 percent of the time, it has nothing to do with the person who feels disrespected. People with high self-worth and good character treat people well. People with low self-worth and weak character treat people poorly. It reveals everything about them, not you. Leo Buscaglia said, "Only the weak are cruel. Gentleness can only be expected from the strong." And a weak person shouldn't be affecting what you feel about yourself.

When you apply the principles in this book, the objective is not coldness or cruelty. Fact: Men enjoy being curious. Fact: They enjoy a little bit of suspense. Another fact: There is nothing cruel or mean about it. If they cannot tell where you're coming from and don't always know what you will do next, they respect you more and treat you better. And that opens up avenues for him to become attached and fall for you.

DESIRABILITY PRINCIPLE 88

When she is less tolerant of mistreatment and has her wits about her, a man will be less likely to try to "condition" her to receive less.

A side-by-side comparison:

EMOTIONAL INTENSITY . . . VERSUS	HINT OF INDIFFERENCE . . .
If he senses you are 100% hooked within the first month . . .	If he senses you're curious and willing to learn more, and you aren't following the pattern that most women follow . . .
. . . he will think he has complete control. That makes him lose interest and see you less often.	. . . he thinks: "Gee, I wonder why she's not buying into it?"
. . . then he'll begin to see what he can get away with. If he behaves in a less-than-gentlemanly way, he assumes you'll forgive him.	. . . then he'll begin to see you as an individual and a real person— not just male entertainment. He'll begin to see, "There is a lot more here." That keeps his interest.

He wants to know if you live in a fairy tale and want to grow up to be a "princess"—or whether you are independent and level-headed, with goals of your own. Men size women up and feel women out. When a man sees you keep your distance ever-so-slightly, and you are outside his reach—and that you don't give him a "free pass"—that hooks him and keeps him interested. He gets hooked when he doesn't have the mental "pull" he's used to having because he has not yet won. That's when it becomes a mental challenge and *more* enjoyable for him, *not less*. "I have to be a better man to get and keep this one." That's how you get a proper courtship.

DESIRABILITY PRINCIPLE 89

The most important thing is to break the pattern of what he's used to seeing.

. . . which unfortunately, is a woman who is used to doing some "unholy compromising" in order to secure a relationship.

Some women try to communicate their strategy, and approach these issues verbally. The next letter illustrates one way that this can backfire.

> *Dear Sherry,*
>
> *I have my own career and my own life. Men see this. And I tell them I will not tolerate bullshit of any kind. And I express that I want to be able to be who I am. I want to be able to show what makes me happy and sad. I want to be able to talk about everything and anything. Wouldn't the right guy want me to be myself? I am a strong woman. But men often seem intimidated by me.*
>
> ### Anonymous Nice Girl

Men are not afraid of strong women. A man named Michael explained, "Men are not afraid of strong women, they are afraid of a woman with very strong jaw muscles and overly-active vocal cords." In other words, no guy wants a woman who will be a "buster" of his private parts. Then he told a story:

> *"A lot of women don't realize that their own worst enemy is their mouth. If she whines and complains a lot, it doesn't matter if she's the most beautiful woman in the world. (Translation? No emotional control.) I remember a blind date where I picked up a woman and started driving to meet two other couples at a restaurant forty minutes*

away. The whole way to the restaurant my date kept saying, 'I'm hungry. I'm starved. I'm hungry. I'm starved. How much longer is it going to be?' She knew where the restaurant was, and how long it would take to get there. But she nagged the whole way and didn't stop venting her discomfort. I decided before we got to the restaurant that I'd never take her out again."

To a man, the worst kind of partner is the one to whom—no matter what he gives—it will never be good enough. The less you telegraph or dictate verbally, the better. The more you talk, the less you can read what he's doing and where he's coming from. You get a lot further by "flying below radar" and playing up your feminine side. Your feminine side disarms men because they have no defense to it. Men are not afraid of strong women . . . they are put off by women who have *lost their femininity*.

Dolly Parton, who is one of the most successful businesswomen and well-respected songwriters in Nashville, said something interesting in a *60 Minutes* interview recently. She said: *"A lot of men thought I was as silly as I looked. I look like a woman but I think like a man. And in this world of business, that has helped me a lot. Because by the time they think that I don't know what's going on . . . I done got the money, and gone."*

Her femininity keeps her stealth. She stays ahead of the game by flying below radar.

DESIRABILITY PRINCIPLE 90

As a general rule, don't telegraph or announce what you want. Not only do you communicate your strategy, you also reduce the mystery in the relationship.

If you don't like what you see, raise the issue when it comes up. If his response is not acceptable, then leave. But don't telegraph to a guy *up front* (who you barely know) what makes you happy or what makes you upset. If you do, many men will use the information to manipulate you. He'll do what you like just long enough to get what he wants. Or, he'll do it to get forgiveness for something he's done wrong.

This is how that plays out . . .

Dear Sherry,

I've been dating a guy on and off. It seems like a vicious cycle. We have been on this insane merry-go-ride for two years. We are very passionate in bed, but outside the bed he is emotionally unavailable and the relationship is not progressing. I have left him a million times only for him to chase me with e-mails, phone calls, and showing up at my home or work. He tells me "this time will be different" and he is "going to change." He begs me not to leave him and tells me he needs me. I take him back and he is good for a day or two then goes back to his selfish ways. I do love him but this emotional merry-go-round is making me dizzy.

Anonymous Nice Girl

If there are any men reading this scenario, they are green with envy. "Man, all that great sex . . . for free?"

He's not "hot and cold" because he's indecisive. He's "hot and cold" because he is manipulating the woman, and keeping his options open. Let's define the "hot and cold" relationship.

DESIRABILITY PRINCIPLE 91

If a relationship is on-and-off within the first year, that's an immediate sign you are wasting your time.

If you think, "If only we can reconnect and sleep together. Then it will escalate into a relationship," you are helping him manipulate you. When a guy you've known a while calls once a week, you can't think, "Yay! My plan is finally working." Because what he's saying to himself is, "Cool, this one I can sleep with every two weeks," and then he tries to find another woman he can sleep with in between. What I often hear from women is: "But I really want this guy. We had great chemistry. How can I spike his interest?" They are just not willing to accept that "this guy" is manipulating them, or *that that is who he is*.

The question I often hear from women is, "How do I stop thinking about him? How do I stop caring so much?" If you are on a diet, you can't think about chocolate cake constantly, right? Same goes for relationships. Many women are so gripped with fear over the loss of a man that they think of him constantly. Stopping that unhealthy obsession solves 90 percent of the problem, and lifts all the pain. When you are no longer obsessed, men sense it. You often get what you want. This gives the power back to you.

If you want to control your emotions, you have to control your thoughts. As Eleanor Roosevelt said, "You must do the thing you think you cannot do."

DESIRABILITY PRINCIPLE 92

The best chance at success with a particular guy is when you are not intensely attached.

Whether you are starting a relationship and you want to keep your feet on the ground, or you are ending one and need to detach, the following exercise will help. The key is to stop thinking about him altogether—cold turkey.

How to Stop Thinking about Him

- Whenever you think about him, STOP.
- Consciously replace the thought of him with another thought or activity.
- It must be a feel-good thought or activity.
- The key is to distract yourself, immediately.
- Do this repeatedly, each time he pops into your head.
- Get creative. Immediately turn on your favorite show, eat your favorite meal, go to the gym, or get out for a walk.
- Each and every time you think of him—without

exception—stop the worry and pain and force yourself to experience the opposite. Do something that feels good.

If you are at work, get your favorite coffee. If you are in the car, put in a feel-good CD. When children cry, you distract them with a toy, right? You have to break the downward spiral of negativity and force yourself to focus on positive things that have *nothing to do with him*. If you do this ten times a day for a few days, you will break the habit of obsessing over him. That is how you lift the pain and pull yourself back up by your own bootstraps.

In *Paradise Lost*, John Milton wrote, "The mind is its own place, and in itself can make a heaven of hell, a hell of heaven." In Chapter 2 we talked about not seeing a new guy all the time or for too many consecutive nights in a row. And readers follow this advice. Where they screw up is that while they are not in his company, they think about the guy constantly—and form an unhealthy dependence. You may as well move in with him the first week if you are going to think of him twenty-four hours a day.

While you detach, always re-evaluate your "prize." If he still isn't giving you what you want, the question to ask yourself is whether you really want him. Maybe he's a bratty child in an adult body and never went through the rites of passage from "boy" to "man" . . . and his mamma still does his laundry, which gives him a false sense of grandiosity. When you encounter a guy like that, don't assume you are no longer desirable. You have to get up, dust yourself off, and say, "He isn't the person

I thought he was. I need to dust myself off and invest my energy elsewhere." As Maya Angelou said, "When people show you who they are, believe them . . . the *first* time."

DESIRABILITY PRINCIPLE 93

**A good man is not thinking, "How can I take?"
He's thinking, "How can I give?"**

A quality man wants to keep his wife or girlfriend happy—emotionally. It's ego: "I am *man enough* to please my woman!" That makes him feel like a stud. Now let's define happy: Happiness is not getting scraps.

Don't take it personally. Very little has anything to do with you. Many people lack the basic equipment to be in a relationship and there's nothing you can do to change it. You can't take a skunk and dip it in perfume and hope it becomes a puppy. Eventually, the perfume will wear off and you'll still have a skunk on your hands.

Always look at who you are dealing with; what you see is what you get. His character won't change. His career might change, his clothing might change, his priorities might change, his residence might change. But his character will stay the same.

The men who think it's okay to give scraps to you lack this basic equipment necessary for a good relationship. Another way of explaining this is by comparing it to going to the dentist. It doesn't matter how wonderful the dentist is, if the patient is terrified of dentists. If you feel rejected by someone, it may have little to do with you.

Everyone has to bring certain equipment to the table.

What Is the Basic Emotional Equipment?

- Character and decency
- A stand-up person
- Consideration for others
- Appreciation for kindness
- A sense of proportion with respect to how much a person gives, and how much they take
- Loyalty to those who are loyal to you

I remember that a teacher of mine once said, "Make those people important . . . those people who make you important." It's not that hard, if everyone makes an effort. And if it's become hard, and you feel like a slave laborer in this relationship, stop punishing yourself. Misery is not a return. You have full control over how you are made to feel. You may feel like you are handcuffed and bound—but you are holding the key to those cuffs and can very easily take them off.

If you are seeing a guy for several months, and you allow him to see you once a week—for sex—and on top of that you are wanting more from the relationship, you are signaling to him that he can take advantage of you. Sex is not something you do to reward someone or to score a relationship. Sex is something you do with a man who already cares about you. If months have gone by and you aren't talking at least every other day, that's not a relationship. This is often when the nice girl instinct kicks into overdrive. Here's the succession of logic:

> *"He was wonderful in the beginning."*
> *"I must have screwed things up."*
> *"I need to . . . do more . . . work harder . . . jump higher . . . and pick up a two-by-four and beat myself up with it by wearing myself out and telling myself I'm not worthy."*

Life is hard enough; you don't need anyone around darkening your doorstep to make it worse. It's not always you. Maybe it's just not a good fit. Maybe he just doesn't have the basic equipment (and nor will he with *any* woman).

So remember, have a wait-and-see attitude and, while you learn about him, keep a parachute on your heart. With a good guy, if you regulate or slow down what you give early on, you will see what kind of person you are dealing with. The cream will rise to the top. When you give a little and then wait to see what comes back, the guy who is worth having around will give also. If he cools off, a hint of indifference acts as a trigger. He will be concerned about what you are feeling. A woman can tell how much a man cares by how much he remembers what she likes, and whether he's doing things to make her happy.

That's the big picture: your happiness. And health. You should never care what a man thinks of you—*until he demonstrates to you that he cares about making you happy*. If he isn't trying to make you happy, then send him back from "whence" he came because winning him over will have no benefit. At the end of the day, happiness, joy, . . . and yes . . . your "emotional stability" . . . those comprise the only measuring stick you really need to have.

8

FROM "I MIGHT" TO
"I Do"

How to Have the Delicate Conversations About Engagement and Marriage

Protect yourself so that nobody overrides you, overrules you, or steps on you. Just say, "Just a minute. I'm worth everything, dear."

~MAYA ANGELOU

Stepping off the Marry-Go-Round

In a perfect world, Romeo meets Juliet. After a year of a whirlwind courtship, he rents a Lear jet, flies her to a private island, and drops to one knee and proposes. Then fireworks light up the sky, the planets align, birds are chirping, dogs and cats go skipping into the sunset, and everybody goes home happy.

Reality check: More often than not, proposals don't happen like they do in the movies. You may get a good ring, or a good proposal, but they don't always come together (unless he's got a great scriptwriter, or has spent a lot of time in the Hallmark aisle). Sometimes there's no fanfare at all. Behind closed doors the guy is saying, "All right, all right. We'll go look at rings, I promise. There's two minutes left in the game. Can we discuss this another time?"

Ever notice that men act funny when a jewelry commercial comes on? The reason men hate these ads is that they can literally feel the tension thicken in the room. *"For Valentine's Day, show her that you love her. Diamonds are forever."* Then they show a woman beaming with joy, with sappy music in the background. Then the bride and groom running down the beach in their gown and tux. *"May your love last as long as the diamond does."* After the commercial is over, his girlfriend is looking down at her left hand with a sad pouty face, like a little girl who dropped her ice cream cone. Like a cartoon, an imaginary bubble pops up over her head. "Where the hell is my ring?" Meanwhile, the bubble over his head reads, "Which Madison Avenue asshole decided to interrupt my playoffs with this crap?"

Since most women generally are at a loss to find the right language to talk about engagement, this chapter will help you improve your skills in that area. The information you are about to read is based on the feedback I gathered from a number of men who have either recently gotten engaged or are already married. The first thing all men unanimously agreed on was the following:

DESIRABILITY PRINCIPLE 94

You have a much better chance of getting engaged when a man doesn't feel pressured into it.

When it comes to the "negotiations," the bitch's approach works better than the typical nice girl's attempts to get a proposal. The bitch doesn't pout. She doesn't hint. She doesn't nag. For a whole year, there is none of that. She goes out, has fun, and doesn't tip her hand or discuss commitment. Why? Because a year or so later, he is attached. He is powerfully hooked. He finds her desirable to be around. She doesn't represent pressure . . . or an obligation. She is a prize he worked for and won . . . almost. All of this gives her clout.

The bitch's approach is subtle, for two reasons. First, she understands that guys aren't stupid. He doesn't have to be the spelling-bee champ to understand that most women wouldn't exactly consider the relationship a smashing success if they simply lived with a guy for years on end. Unless he was raised by a pack of wolves, he knows this much.

The second reason she keeps her approach subtle is that if it's been a year, asking him "Where is this going?" is moot. If he hasn't brought it up, asked you to marry him, or given a serious indication that he's going to soon, it's crystal clear where it's *going*: He is trying to have his cake and eat it too.

A newlywed named Jeff explained:

> *"I'd lived with other women before I got married to my wife.*
>
> *And all guys know that after a year or two at the most, the woman loses a bit of her dignity. And truthfully, you lose respect for the woman if she stays, because on some level the guy knows the relationship has become a free ride. He knows he's getting all the perks without giving anything up. If the woman wants to get married and he's stalling for a couple of years, he knows he's taking advantage of the woman.*
>
> *Or he knows he can ride it out, until he's ready to leave. If she is willing to stick around, the guy is thinking, 'Oh good, I don't have to marry her.' But then you begin to think, 'Why is she letting me have a free ride?' There is something wrong with her."*

In other words, he begins to lose respect. He assumes she is naïve . . . or desperate. She becomes less appealing because he knows he's taking advantage of her and she's not standing up for herself. As they say in Hollywood, "They'll kill you with encouragement."

This is often when the devaluing process begins. "Why do I need to prize and cherish her?" An even more basic assumption lies below this one: "I have the option to keep her until I get tired of her. Or until something better comes along. I'll enjoy this until I feel like going back to my bachelor life." And this is precisely the level of security a bitch will not allow a man to have.

DESIRABILITY PRINCIPLE 95

The bitch won't allow herself to be with a man who is biding his time until something better comes along.

This directly relates to why men marry bitches. *A bitch has strength of conviction.* As painful as it is, as afraid as she might feel—she will leave if she doesn't get what she wants. And guess what? That's precisely why she gets what she wants. When a bitch *subtly* gets the point across that she *won't* wait forever, it becomes the same as any other negotiation. When one person is willing to walk off the showroom floor, the other person has to come up with a better offer.

That said, you can't give him an ultimatum. But here's what you can do: You can have one or two conversations with him. The first conversation is a fact-gathering session. And if you don't like what you hear, in the second conversation you lower the boom.

If it's been a year and you want him to propose, the first conversation should be one where you are very matter-of-fact. Say something like:

> *"We've been going out for a year. I love you and think you are wonderful. And I accept things as they are. But I'd like a little bit more from a relationship than what we have right now and this doesn't really seem to be progressing."*

(Then, be silent.)

The less you say after that, the more power you will have. The objective is to create a nonthreatening opening for him in a very casual way. Your job is to keep a poker face and show no emotion. Why? You want to get the truth. You don't want lip service or to be told what he thinks you want to hear—you want to get his *real* answer. He may tell you he's madly in love with you and he's been planning a surprise. Then he might hint about going away for the weekend. Or, he might ask if you want to shop for a ring.

If he doesn't give you the answer you want to hear, and you get a vibe that he's avoiding the subject at all costs, that's your cue to become scarce. Whatever time you normally spend with him, cut that back 60 to 70 percent. See him once or twice in a two-week period. Then plan a weekend getaway with the girls. (That always petrifies them because they don't know what your friends might tell you.) If he asks you whom you are seeing, assure him you aren't seeing anyone else. Just keep yourself busy and outside his reach. But don't explain why. *He will know.*

DESIRABILITY PRINCIPLE 96

A strong woman does not hint about marriage or ask, "Where is this going?" Instead, she hints about the removal of herself from the relationship.
The word marriage *never even comes up.*

Rest assured, he'll get it. Within a couple of weeks, it's likely that another conversation will come up because he will notice a change and ask you, "What's wrong?" When he does, you don't want to seem as though you are let down, devastated, or upset. If he is still not telling you he wants the relationship to move forward, you may want to consider telling him the following:

> *"We've had a wonderful time. And I don't regret the time we've spent together. I think the world of you. But obviously we want different things, so we need to do the right thing. I love you and I want you to be happy, I want you to have what you are looking for also. I think it's time for us to move on."*

This is when you have to be classy and show him that you are different. No late-night drama. No crying. No guilt trips. No martyr or victim on the premises. Don't give him the impression that you feel you've been short-changed. And don't have any further conversations with him. This is not a beg-a-thon.

The reason silence is golden at this point is that anything you say after that will let him know he can buy time, stall, or "okeydoke" you. Any weeping or crying in a discussion like this will show him you are unsure, and he'll think he doesn't have to change a thing. *What it tells him is you can be manipulated and he doesn't have to take you seriously.*

Simply emphasize what you want, and then appear strong and mature. "I don't want you getting into something that you are not ready for." If you are calm, it scares a man far more, because then he knows it's not a hormone-driven decision. You've based it on what he's offering, who he is, and what he has shown you he is willing to contribute. And you don't intend to settle because you don't see yourself as desperate. This raises your stock. "Uh-oh. I have to give her a reason to stay, or I will lose her." Now let's recap:

- He doesn't get an ultimatum.
- He doesn't get pressure, hear "marry me, marry me," or have the feeling he's being tied up like a Thanksgiving turkey.
- You are mature, open, honest, and nonjudgmental.
- You aren't shooting the relationship down, expressing anger that he's "milking the cow for free," or telling him he screwed up.
- You simply said, "You are fun, neat, and cool, and I love you. But before we waste any more of each other's time, we need to get this thing figured out."

It's not what you say, it's *how you hold yourself when you leave*. That's what Kate Middleton, the Duchess of Cambridge did when she and her husband, Prince William, took a "break" from dating, before they got married. It was reported she kept a "stiff upper lip." She was seen out dancing and having fun, but conducted herself in a dignified way publicly. Shortly thereafter, they reconciled and got engaged.

You have to hold yourself with a calm that is unlikely given the circumstances. Then he thinks, "Hmmm. This one is a cat of a different breed." Then you become irreplaceable. It's all about character, and it's all about class.

Men are socialized to believe that women are the weaker sex. So when you are willing to stand on your principles even though it might be painful or it might cost you something, you become the ultimate warrior. "Wait a minute. I had her. Now I can't get my way with her. What's going on here?" When you can pull back, collect yourself, and act like you are aware of what's going on, guess who comes out on top?

This is what most men are looking for in a wife. This is their ultimate dream girl—a feminine woman who is not ruled by emotions and insecurity. There's a quiet dignity about certain women. It's like a force field around her that melts him like butter. She doesn't scream. She doesn't shout. Her subdued self-worth and faith in herself is the true essence of what makes her a bitch.

Jessica and Rick are a perfect example of this dynamic. They were together for three years and had a great relationship. Nevertheless, he was dragging his feet with respect to marriage.

Jessica then said, "If you don't want to marry me after three years, we should go our separate ways. Bye-bye." I remember her telling me this story and waving her hand as she said "Bye-bye." Then she cut off all contact. Three months later, Rick called Jessica and asked, "Can I see you for dinner tomorrow night. Please?" She declined. He kept persisting every night. She finally agreed, reluctantly. At dinner, he proposed with a beauty of a ring.

It's how men think. If a quarterback gets sacked and leveled by a very hard hit, he'll get back up. It won't faze him, and he'll still try to throw his touchdowns.

If you are backing away and he asks, "Can we still see each other sometimes?" tell him, "Of course." Then, every time he wants to see you, be unavailable to see him. Take your time with him from 60 to 70 percent available down to a 97 percent unavailable. Avoid him *without* the appearance of doing so. This will allow his imagination to run wild. That's when the loneliness and the lack of companionship will begin to set in.

What you *don't* want to do is talk openly about seeing other men. Why? No need. He will already be petrified at the thought of another man penetrating his woman. "Another guy is going to deliver something I can't deliver?" Then he will start envisioning you being serenaded and serviced by some other man (who might do it better), which will be enough to drive him over the edge. He's been sleeping with you for a year, and in his mind you were built just for him. The thought of another man is . . . *unthinkable*. This is why you have to make yourself scarce, so that the *unthinkable* starts to be *thought* about over and over . . . to the degree that it keeps him up nights. That's when he'll make a beeline to the nearest jewelry shop.

Every man *thinks* he wants his freedom . . . that is, until he gets it. Then, separation anxiety coupled with meeting a woman in a bar who says, "What kind of car do you drive?" makes him realize he's losing the best thing he's ever had.

I call this my "beer nuts analogy." If you are a good woman, you represent his relationship diet. You are a healthy breakfast, lunch, and dinner. Some other girl he might get attention from represents beer nuts. And as long he gets three meals a day at home, he can grab a little attention, or a few beer nuts, with a cold beer with the guys. But when you remove yourself from the equation altogether, he has to make three meals out of beer nuts. That's when he quickly realizes the grass isn't so green on the other side. "Hey, these are crappy beer nuts."

Remember, you want to take the high road. Don't subtly threaten him that you will be dating other men, because it goes without saying. He will feel like you are trying to hold something over his head: "Do what I say, or else." To some men, this is terribly offensive. "If I don't get what I want when I want it, I'll throw everything we had away in a heartbeat." That makes it seem like the relationship may not be worth "forever."

Jane and Darren were dating and she gave him a direct ultimatum after one year. Two weeks later, he stopped by and was going to propose. And when he came in, she proceeded to show him all the e-mails she was getting from a guy she had already gone out with a few times. She did not know at the time that he had a ring in his pocket. Although he was devastated, he saw it as a sign that the relationship wasn't worthy of forever.

At the end of the day, your character and willingness to stand by your convictions are all he can really rely on. He knows that the wrong woman can ruin him emotionally and financially. When a bitch stands up for what she believes in a decent and honest way, it brings all his emotions to the surface. The relationship becomes very real. There is a genuineness and an authenticity about her. By being willing to tell him, "I'm putting it all on the line and I'm willing to walk out on comfort and security to get what it is I truly want," he'll often feel that he needs the woman. He can't exist without her. That's when she becomes "the one."

DESIRABILITY PRINCIPLE 97

When you stand up for yourself in a dignified, feminine, and womanly way, you can get *anything* you want from a man. When you place a high value on yourself *in the right way*, so will he.

Sometimes it takes minutes for him to come around, other times it takes weeks or months. If he's in love with you he will come around. And if he doesn't, *he would have wasted your time for five years or ten years* and you would have ended up with the exact same outcome. *So you lost nothing.*

So give the guy a chance to propose. After all, men aren't predisposed or conditioned to think about marriage.

He's not lying in bed at night dreaming of a gondola ride for two in Italy, with both of you being serenaded by a guy with a thick accent singing "O Solo Mio," to the strum of a little guitar. However, a year has gone by and now he's attached. And now you are not so easily replaced or forgotten.

Whereas women fall in love in a man's presence, men tend to realize they are in love in a woman's absence. And sometimes all he needs is a little time to make that realization.

Changing the Lens You See Yourself Through

In one of her diary entries, Marilyn Monroe wrote that when she was walking down the street with Joe DiMaggio, she felt like he should walk on the inside of the curb and she should "walk in the gutter." She was arguably the most beautiful woman in the world—a legend. And even with all her beauty and sex appeal, she had the nagging feeling that many nice girls share because of low self-worth—like an anchor is dragging them down in life.

When choosing a wife, men notice whether you are happy. Or, whether you feel good about yourself. Michelle and Michael are happily married, and when they were dating she said something to him that he remembered years later: "If I'm married, I'm going to be very happy. And if I'm single I'm going to live a great life and be happy also. So it's not really a priority." This is precisely what a bitch brings to a relationship that an insecure "nice girl" does not. A joy of life . . . a joie de vivre.

What is the difference between Michelle, an ordinary woman, and the legendary Marilyn Monroe? It boils down to this:

DESIRABILITY PRINCIPLE 98

In life, half the battle has to do with the lens you choose to see yourself through. Your fulfillment hinges on whether you see yourself through a positive lens or a negative one.

If you don't feel like you are "enough" *without* a husband, you will not feel like you are "enough" with a husband. If you see yourself through a negative lens, you will tell yourself things like, "What's wrong with me? All my friends are married . . . *except me*." Being single doesn't make you less than . . . any more than marriage is a guarantee for happiness. If that were the case, half the marriages wouldn't end in divorce.

However, seeing yourself through a positive lens is the best chance at happiness you've got. Enjoy every day. Live it to the fullest. Be positive. Love yourself. And screw what anyone else thinks if they don't approve of you. Don't let anyone darken your doorstep. Otherwise, when you get married, you will still be unhappy and, like Marilyn Monroe, you will feel like you belong in the gutter.

As you have heard from men throughout this book, a man desires . . . craves . . . and holds out for a strong, spirited woman who knows who she is. He doesn't want to feel like he's adopting an orphan or taking in a needy child who apologizes for her need, can't speak her mind, and needs someone else to tell her if she's worthy. So don't think about "happy endings" . . . think about a happy beginning. And start that today . . . regardless of your marital status.

Why does this make you more likely to find a husband? A married man named Mark explained, "Men know that if a woman isn't happy with herself, if he marries her he will become the recipient of her disillusionment, and resentment. It will become 'all his fault' that she's not a happy person. This is why men are instinctively drawn to a woman who is happy with him . . . or without him."

It's why men marry bitches: A guy will be less likely to worry about losing his freedom to a woman who doesn't appear to need him to make her happy.

Of course, this is isn't what women are taught. In the movie *The Joy Luck Club*, there's a scene that typifies the self-abnegating, doting behavior that Rose uses to win her husband over, not understanding why it's having the opposite effect. "I told myself that was the loving way. Over time, I could see that Ted was becoming bored. *So I tried harder*." Then it cuts to a scene in which she and her husband have a discussion about what they'll be having for dinner (which is painful for him because she's become silent to everyone . . . including herself).

Rose: Honey, should we eat in, or go out to eat tonight?

Ted: You decide.

Rose: If we eat in I have lamb chops. Or I could call Square One. I didn't mean to interrupt your work.

Ted: You're not interrupting me. Really I meant what I said. I want to hear what *you* want.

Rose: You've had a hard day and I don't really care. I just want you to be happy . . . Honey, what's wrong?

Ted: It's just that once in a while I'd like to hear what you want. I'd like to hear *your* voice, even if we disagree. You used to be different. You used to have an opinion.

In other words, she used to seem more alive inside. She cared about her own joy. She enjoyed the little things. She wasn't like a broken animal who had served others for so long that she forgot about her own feelings.

Notice how apologetic she is, or how afraid she is to impose. She sees herself as an imposition . . . as lower than him. That is her lens. Later, when she changes that lens, she gets a backbone and her husband's respect reignites.

Dignity and joy go hand in hand. If you feel dignified, you enjoy life more.

In a magazine article, Meg Ryan said, "In my everyday life, I find myself apologizing for a need . . . or the way I feel about something. I don't want to live like that anymore." And I submit to you that you shouldn't either.

DESIRABILITY PRINCIPLE 99

Men don't take it as a compliment when you bend over backward. Men want to feel special, and when you are *too nice* he feels ordinary, because he assumes you'd acquiesce and become a yes-person with *any man*.

Just like women compare physical beauty against other women, men compare their prowess with other men also. When you give him anything too easily, including sleep with him on the first date, he assumes you've done it with every other man as well. Anything he didn't have to work for is something other men can easily get to also. If it's not evidence of his prowess, it is not considered as special. That's why getting something difficult turns them on.

Most "nice girls" are given the opposite information. They are taught the following:

- "If I show him I love him every few hours, it will sink in and he'll love me more."
- "If I 'go along to get along,' he'll think we are more compatible."
- "If I sacrifice myself, I will better our relationship."
- "If I always agree with him, he'll think more highly of my opinions."
- "If I look good, I'll get the respect I want."
- "If I double my efforts, it will double his appreciation."

Then she pleases him right out the door. A man will lose respect and be less likely (not more) to commit whenever he senses that:

- His decision is the final say.
- He is the authoritative figure in the relationship.
- He can do no wrong in your eyes.
- You assume an inferior place in the relationship.

You will never prove to a man that you are the best thing to happen to him by bowing down or compromising yourself. Nor will you prove you are more "worthy" by kissing a man's ass . . . because *then you won't have his respect.* Deep down, men don't find it emotionally fulfilling to be in a relationship that makes him feel as if he's being idolized by an underling.

DESIRABILITY PRINCIPLE 100

He doesn't marry a woman who puts him on a throne. He marries a strong and unique woman whom he can share all of life's special moments with.

A man wants to feel like he is your hero. Men need to feel validated. He wants to feel that you admire him, look up to him, and that he is the protective one in the relationship. *But he wants that from a self-respecting woman who has a backbone and who first and foremost loves herself.*

Ultimately, it's not about him. It's about enjoying your life, with or without him. When you are happy and whole, when your moral compass is dead center, when you are kind to others but demand that they be kind in return . . . you attract the same.

It doesn't happen neatly. You don't have to be perfect. Simply begin with changing your lens . . . and insist on being around quality people. Change the way you see yourself, be careful of those who try to convince you of who you are. If they can convince you that you are ugly when you are beautiful . . . that you are stupid when you are smart . . . that you are incapable when you are capable . . . they can also convince you that you are not worthy when you really are. So don't believe what anyone tells you about yourself. When you do, if their view of you is negative . . . you lose your own feelings and your opinions. You become afraid to approach . . . afraid to be bold . . . afraid to pursue new heights. You become silent to everyone . . . including yourself. You become like a broken horse who is living in bondage, to service others. And that's how you lose the most precious commodity you have to bring to a marriage—you.

Before we end, I think it's important to do one last thing. Let's rewrite the fairy tale, shall we? Let's forget everything we learned in Cinderella, Sleeping Beauty, and Dorothy, Toto, and the Land of Oz—and let's give the fairy tale a little makeover. The storybook ending should read like this:

Once upon a time there was a princess. Along came a prince who asked her if she'd like to ride on his white horse. She said, "I'd like to take a ride on your horse, but I can't right now because I'm a little busy getting my own horse. Go ride off into the sunset without me, and I'll catch up to you a little later." Suddenly, the prince is dumbfounded. He has never seen anything like this before. He has a white horse and a big castle, but the princess isn't in a hurry to move in. She doesn't need him. She has goals of her own. This starts a fire in him that he can't put out. He becomes fixated. One day, he is out galloping on his white horse and something clicks inside him. And he says to himself, "I have to be with her for the rest of my life."

Then they fall in love, marry, and ride off into the sunset. And then she tortures him . . . *lovingly ever after.*

The End

DESIRABILITY
Principles

DESIRABILITY PRINCIPLE 1
In romance, there is nothing more attractive than a woman who has confidence in who she is.

DESIRABILITY PRINCIPLE 2
The woman who is unforgettably sexy is a confident woman who can function on her own, and who won't always let him have the upper hand.

DESIRABILITY PRINCIPLE 3
He needs to see you are smart and feminine, but that you don't need anyone else to think for you.

DESIRABILITY PRINCIPLE 4
Men handle you with more caution (and respect) when they can't figure you out and when they can't read you.

DESIRABILITY PRINCIPLE 5
One way to become much more interesting to a man on a date is to ask him intelligent questions about himself.

DESIRABILITY PRINCIPLE 6
He doesn't marry a woman who is perfect. He marries the woman who is *interesting*.

DESIRABILITY PRINCIPLE 7
The fastest way to become boring to a man is to try to be like everyone else.

DESIRABILITY PRINCIPLE 8
A guy doesn't want to be the only reason a woman feels happy. It's a huge responsibility, and men hate responsibility.

DESIRABILITY PRINCIPLE 9
A quality man will respect a woman who does not tolerate disrespect. This increases his desire and respect for her.

DESIRABILITY PRINCIPLE 10
When a woman gives too much too soon, she sets the groundwork for a one-sided relationship.

DESIRABILITY PRINCIPLE 11
When a man sees you are happy with him *but you can be just as happy without him*, he will take you much more seriously.

DESIRABILITY PRINCIPLE 12
Every guy knows he can find a girl who is simply satisfied with satisfying *him*. They are much more turned on by a woman who cares about her own pleasure as well.

DESIRABILITY PRINCIPLE 13
When you are happy, you are sexy.

DESIRABILITY PRINCIPLE 14
If a woman is indecisive about little things, he will see it as a sign of weakness, and an indicator that she won't be able to make more important decisions later in life.

DESIRABILITY PRINCIPLE 15
Don't believe what anyone tells you about yourself.

DESIRABILITY PRINCIPLE 16
Men like to be curious. They like to feel that there's more to the story than what they already know.

DESIRABILITY PRINCIPLE 17
If you let on that you are insecure about winning him over, he will know he has you. And if he knows he has you, it's unlikely you will engender that overwhelming feeling of attraction that is necessary for him to want to marry you.

DESIRABILITY PRINCIPLE 18
The mental challenge is not, "Can I get her to sleep with me?" The mental challenge is, "Can I get *and keep* her attention?"

DESIRABILITY PRINCIPLE 19
As soon as a man has his guard up, he will not fall in love or get attached.

DESIRABILITY PRINCIPLE 20
Your power gets lost the minute you start asking, "Where do I stand?" Because what you've just told him is that the terms of the relationship are now *his to dictate*.

DESIRABILITY PRINCIPLE 21
**He needs to see that you are smart,
but that you aren't talking.**

DESIRABILITY PRINCIPLE 22
**When a woman rushes in too quickly, a man will
assume she is in love with a "fantasy" or the *idea* of
having a relationship. But if he has to slowly win her
over, incrementally, he'll think she's falling in love
with *who he is*.**

DESIRABILITY PRINCIPLE 23
**Don't even mention the word *commitment*. *That's the
whole trick*. The less you say about it, the closer you
are to getting one.**

DESIRABILITY PRINCIPLE 24
**If he has no guarantees, becomes attached, and
thinks you could be gone at any time, that's when
he'll cherish the idea of securing a relationship.**

DESIRABILITY PRINCIPLE 25
**There's nothing more prized to a man than some-
thing he had to wait for, work for, or struggle a little
bit to get.**

DESIRABILITY PRINCIPLE 26
As soon as a woman hands a man a more serious commitment on a silver platter, he'll be reluctant to take it.

DESIRABILITY PRINCIPLE 27
The whole art of seduction involves the appearance of slight elusiveness.

DESIRABILITY PRINCIPLE 28
You want to figure out his pattern, but don't let him figure out yours.

DESIRABILITY PRINCIPLE 29
Men are far more smitten when they feel like they are "stealing" your time away from something else you could have been doing.

DESIRABILITY PRINCIPLE 30
When a woman makes a man feel he's trusted, it makes him feel strong and worthy. It makes him want to be honorable and do the right thing.

DESIRABILITY PRINCIPLE 31
Men like rules and they like guidelines. If there's something you don't like, a quality guy will respect you for voicing your opinion. He wants to know what the "dos and don'ts" are.

DESIRABILITY PRINCIPLE 32
Men love knowing there's a small part of you that they can't get to.

DESIRABILITY PRINCIPLE 33
Men read a lot into where you've been, by how dolled up you are when you get home. If you are dolled up and you weren't with him, it will keep him wondering a little.

DESIRABILITY PRINCIPLE 34
The second you put your life on hold, you become less interesting.

DESIRABILITY PRINCIPLE 35
The magic formula is to give a little time and energy to him . . . and then focus on your own life. Give a little . . . and then pull back.

DESIRABILITY PRINCIPLE 36
Women are constantly being told amazing sex will win a man's heart. This is false. Just because a man sleeps with you doesn't mean he cares about you. Nor will good sex *make him care* about you.

DESIRABILITY PRINCIPLE 37
When talking about quality men who are marriage material, a wholesome private "mine only" feeling is something men desire.

DESIRABILITY PRINCIPLE 38
When a man sees you wearing very revealing clothes, he'll often assume you don't have anything else going for you.

DESIRABILITY PRINCIPLE 39
When you are playing for keeps, modest is hottest.

DESIRABILITY PRINCIPLE 40
If he is not willing to wait for sex, he is not worth your time. This is not a man who wants to be kept.

DESIRABILITY PRINCIPLE 41

The way to weed out a quality man from one that is not worthy of your time is his patience about waiting to have sex. If he likes you, he'll be happy just being in your company.

DESIRABILITY PRINCIPLE 42

If you appear cautious, that will come across to a quality guy as though you have high self-worth.

DESIRABILITY PRINCIPLE 43

The purpose of waiting is not just to seem classier. You also want to give yourself time to find out certain important facts about him.

DESIRABILITY PRINCIPLE 44

Who he *tells* you he is in the beginning has very little to do with how he will *treat* you. If there's sex involved, he'll promise you things you've never even heard of.

DESIRABILITY PRINCIPLE 45

What most men are looking for is a woman who is natural in bed and who genuinely enjoys sex with him.

DESIRABILITY PRINCIPLE 46
**Men I spoke with said that they
rarely pay attention to a woman's flaws until
she points them out to him.**

DESIRABILITY PRINCIPLE 47
**A woman who behaves more coolly
and casually after sex *is the exact opposite* of
what he is used to experiencing.**

DESIRABILITY PRINCIPLE 48
**When you aren't mind-blown after sex, and you continue to focus on your own life, he'll start looking at
you differently. Then he'll start wanting to secure a
relationship with you.**

DESIRABILITY PRINCIPLE 49
**After sex, behave as if the
relationship is still new.**

DESIRABILITY PRINCIPLE 50
**Men are intrigued by anything they
do not completely control.**

DESIRABILITY PRINCIPLE 51
When you maintain a bit of privacy and he has to wonder a little where you are, it stimulates his imagination.

DESIRABILITY PRINCIPLE 52
To a man, a long term relationship with long periods of no sex represents a relationship with no love, no affection, and no emotional connection.

DESIRABILITY PRINCIPLE 53
Always preserve the mystery. Keep your sex sporadic and unpredictable. It makes it much more intense for a man.

DESIRABILITY PRINCIPLE 54
When a woman reacts emotionally, men get three things: attention, control, and the feeling of importance.

DESIRABILITY PRINCIPLE 55
When you are easily manipulated, he will assume he doesn't have to give as much in the way of a commitment in order to keep you there.

DESIRABILITY PRINCIPLE 56
**An emotional reaction is always a reward,
even if it's negative attention.**

DESIRABILITY PRINCIPLE 57
Men *hear* what they *see*.

DESIRABILITY PRINCIPLE 58
**When a man tries to make you jealous, it rarely has
anything to do with his desire for someone else.**

DESIRABILITY PRINCIPLE 59
**Once *you* start doing the same thing *he* was doing,
suddenly the bad behavior will magically disappear.**

DESIRABILITY PRINCIPLE 60
**When a man doesn't call, a bunch of scenarios will
run through a woman's mind.
Similarly, his imagination will run wild also.**

DESIRABILITY PRINCIPLE 61
**The more rational and calm you remain, the more
emotional he will become.**

DESIRABILITY PRINCIPLE 62
To a man, it is inappropriate to be emotional when talking about something important. If you speak calmly, he'll assume it's more important.

DESIRABILITY PRINCIPLE 63
Many men reduce women to a set of givens—that women are emotional, and that he'll be able to gain control if he finds her emotional buttons.

DESIRABILITY PRINCIPLE 64
He is testing to see if you believe in yourself. He wants to know who is at the controls. When you aren't easily shaken he sees, "This one can't be manipulated."

DESIRABILITY PRINCIPLE 65
Men may tell you about an alleged imperfection, to trigger your insecurity. If it doesn't trigger your insecurity, it will often trigger his.

DESIRABILITY PRINCIPLE 66
To encourage the right behavior, state what you want, and then give him a way to fix it. Show him how he can be your hero.

DESIRABILITY PRINCIPLE 67
When he's dating you, he'll constantly be on guard and watching to discern, "Does she like me for who I am? Or for what I can provide?"

DESIRABILITY PRINCIPLE 68
When a man sees you are focused on your own dreams or on elevating yourself, he feels safer marrying you because he doesn't worry about what you'll be trying to take *away from him*.

DESIRABILITY PRINCIPLE 69
Men don't judge how much money you have. They notice *how you budget* what you do have.

DESIRABILITY PRINCIPLE 70
Men admire women who want to elevate themselves and pull themselves up by their own bootstraps, and fear women who are social climbers at a man's expense.

DESIRABILITY PRINCIPLE 71
He doesn't want to marry a helpless little girl whom he will have to take care of.

DESIRABILITY PRINCIPLE 72
**For a man, the words *respect* and *trust* are inter-
changeable. If he doesn't respect you, he will not
trust you.**

DESIRABILITY PRINCIPLE 73
**When he gives you something, always acknowledge
the kindness behind the gesture, not the material
item itself.**

DESIRABILITY PRINCIPLE 74
**A man's favorite word is *appreciate*. He wants more
than anything to feel revered and valued. When she's
appreciative, it motivates him to give her the world.**

DESIRABILITY PRINCIPLE 75
**Most men aren't looking for an *equal* contribution,
just a *fair* contribution. By contributing in a reasonable way, you maintain his respect and trust.**

DESIRABILITY PRINCIPLE 76
**If a man feels taken advantage of, he will check out
and there will be no emotional connection.**

DESIRABILITY PRINCIPLE 77

When you move into someone else's place, you don't just give up your personal space and belongings. More important, nearly always you also *lose your feeling of independence*.

DESIRABILITY PRINCIPLE 78

If marriage is extremely important to you and you are ready to set a wedding date, don't move in unless you have a ring and a date.

DESIRABILITY PRINCIPLE 79

The biggest turn-on for a man is knowing that he is in love with a woman he can really count on, who will *really* be there for him.

DESIRABILITY PRINCIPLE 80

A guy who really thinks you could be "the one" will say very little about marriage. He'll slowly open up over the course of several months, because he won't want to scare you off.

DESIRABILITY PRINCIPLE 81

The more control you have over yourself, the more of a hold you will have on his heart.

DESIRABILITY PRINCIPLE 82
**If a man really cares, he feels vulnerable. That's
when he needs a protective shield the most and
that's when he'll often behave more coolly.**

DESIRABILITY PRINCIPLE 83
**Whenever boredom sets in, simply
break the routine. As soon as the routine
changes, it will pique his interest.**

DESIRABILITY PRINCIPLE 84
**When a woman can laugh at herself and doesn't take
things personally, she seems more stable.**

DESIRABILITY PRINCIPLE 85
**Men don't believe they mislead women. Men believe
that women mislead themselves.**

DESIRABILITY PRINCIPLE 86
**If you have the emotional discipline
and self-control, you will have
more control over how you are treated
and how much you are respected.**

DESIRABILITY PRINCIPLE 87
If someone doesn't appear to respect you, don't waste a moment of your time on them.

DESIRABILITY PRINCIPLE 88
When she is less tolerant of mistreatment and has her wits about her, a man will be less likely to try to "condition" her to receive less.

DESIRABILITY PRINCIPLE 89
The most important thing is to break the pattern of what he's used to seeing.

DESIRABILITY PRINCIPLE 90
As a general rule, don't telegraph or announce what you want. Not only do you communicate your strategy, you also reduce the mystery in the relationship.

DESIRABILITY PRINCIPLE 91
If a relationship is on-and-off within the first year, that's an immediate sign you are wasting your time.

DESIRABILITY PRINCIPLE 92
The best chance at success with a particular guy is when you are not intensely attached.

DESIRABILITY PRINCIPLE 93
A good man is not thinking, "How can I take?" He's thinking, "How can I give?"

DESIRABILITY PRINCIPLE 94
You have a much better chance of getting engaged when a man doesn't feel pressured into it.

DESIRABILITY PRINCIPLE 95
The bitch won't allow herself to be with a man who is biding his time until something better comes along.

DESIRABILITY PRINCIPLE 96
A strong woman does not hint about marriage or ask, "Where is this going?" Instead, she hints about the removal of herself from the relationship.
The word* marriage *never even comes up.

DESIRABILITY PRINCIPLE 97
When you stand up for yourself in a dignified, feminine, and womanly way, you can get *anything* you want from a man. When you place a high value on yourself *in the right way*, so will he.

DESIRABILITY PRINCIPLE 98
In life, half the battle has to do with the lens you choose to see yourself through. Your fulfillment hinges on whether you see yourself through a positive lens or a negative one.

DESIRABILITY PRINCIPLE 99
Men don't take it as a compliment when you bend over backward. Men want to feel special, and when you are *too nice* he feels ordinary, because he assumes you'd acquiesce and become a yes-person with *any man*.

DESIRABILITY PRINCIPLE 100
He doesn't marry a woman who puts him on a throne. He marries a strong and unique woman whom he can share all of life's special moments with.

INDEX